Young People and Drugs:
Evaluation and Treatment

About the authors:

James Heaslip, C.C.D.C.R., is manager of the Residential Treatment Services at Hazelden Pioneer House, a treatment facility for chemically dependent young people in Plymouth, Minnesota. He has sixteen years of experience working with chemically dependent young people, and supervises counselors, psychologists, chaplains, and admissions personnel at Pioneer House. He is a noted public speaker and has acted as a consultant on a national level in establishment of treatment facilities. He is also a consultant for continuing education programs at Hazelden. Heaslip was a 1988 nominee for the Irene Whitney Award, which goes to individuals who provide dedicated service in the chemical dependency treatment field.

Dennis L. Hogenson, Ed.D., Ph.D., has twenty-five years experience as a psychologist and specializes in clinical and educational psychology, particularly the evaluation and treatment of adolescent and young adult patients. Among his numerous credentials is a Certificate in Reality Therapy completed with William Glasser at the Institute for Reality Training in Santa Monica, California. He has done significant training and research in special education with particular emphasis on specific learning disabilities including dyslexia. Much of his work has been with personality testing and psychological reporting concerning patients referred to him, ones in his own private practice, and ones in chemical dependency treatment programs.

Della Van Dyke, C.C.D.C.R., has worked in the chemical dependency treatment field since 1976. Since 1980 she has worked at Hazelden Pioneer House specifically with chemically dependent young people. She now supervises a multidisciplinary team on a thirty-two-bed inpatient treatment unit. She is the co-author of two pamphlets published by Hazelden which are used extensively by young adults in treatment.

Lola Vedders is a special education and English teacher at the Highview Alternative Program in New Hope, Minn., for young people who drop out of high school. She has a Masters Degree in Learning Disabilities and licensure in Emotional/Behavioral Disorders from the College of St. Thomas, St. Paul, Minn.

Young People and Drugs: Evaluation and Treatment

James Heaslip, Della Van Dyke,
Dennis Hogenson, with Lola Vedders

With a Foreword by Damian McElrath

First published June 1989.

ISBN: 0-89486-584-6

Library of Congress Catalog Card Number:
88-83962

Printed in the United States of America

Editor's Note:
Hazelden Educational Materials offers a variety of information on chemical dependency and related areas. Our publications do not necessarily represent Hazelden or its programs, nor do they officially speak for any Twelve Step organization.

The stories of people in this book are true. In all cases, names have been changed and in many cases the circumstances have been changed, to protect anonymity.

The following publisher has generously given permission to use extended quotations from copyrighted works: From *Development Through Life: A Psychological Approach,* by Barbara Newman and Philip Newman. Copyright 1984. Published by The Dorsey Press. Reprinted by permission of Brooks-Cole Publishing.

CONTENTS

FOREWORD

The rampant and pervasive spread of alcohol and other drug use, abuse, and dependency throughout the United States has not spared the young people of our country.

Alcohol and other drugs have been on the scene for a long time and in recent times have become readily accessible to our young people. In the 1980s young people have found the means to produce chemicals in makeshift, home-style laboratories. With more chemicals accessible in the future, there is a higher risk and potential for the scourge of chemical dependency to continue spreading among the young.

The many attempts in this decade to respond to the problem, to prevent, educate, intervene, and treat the illness, have largely been uncoordinated at the national, state, and local levels.

Besides the lack of coordination, another factor has partially paralyzed efforts and willingness to undertake a concerted and massive counterattack on the major crisis confronting us. Some professionals and nonprofessionals are reluctant to admit that young people can be chemically dependent, and are even more resistant to labeling them as such.

For some, it's much easier and less painful to talk about acting out or even to suggest mental illness as the problem. These people are leery of deciding that a young person is chemically dependent in part because of the acrimony surrounding such labeling. A sizable group maintains that calling young people chemically dependent may stigmatize and isolate them and increase their deviant behavior. They believe that many kids in treatment programs may be just "typical kids" who got caught.

Another group, just as sizable and vocal, contends that young people can be chemically dependent, and that failure to label them as such allows a usually serious, life-destroying disease to run its course. They fear mislabeling chemical dependency as something else–for example, depression, delinquency, or normative behavior for the age group–would allow this serious consequence come to pass.

These very legitimate concerns–about labeling and mislabeling; about bounty hunting, body snatching, bed filling; about mistaken identity and misplaced persons–have been highlighted in Minnesota in both the private and public sectors since 1981. In that year the Citizen's League Report, commenting on the problem of chemical dependency and Minnesota's response to it, pointed out that young people present special diagnosis and treatment problems. The report stated that though "chemical *abuse* by juveniles often is relatively easy to detect . . . it is much more difficult to diagnose chemical *dependency* in a juvenile.[1]

In this context, it has been difficult and frustrating to devise and coordinate a strategy to assist young people in avoiding or recovering from the illness of chemical dependency.

This book then is indeed timely. It transcends the breast-beating, handwringing, and lamentations about the problem and our inability to do anything about it. The authors spend very little time speculating about the possibility of the illness's existence. Their approach is empirical in the sense that they work with chemically dependent young people every day.

Consequently, the book proceeds straight to the task–diagnosis and treatment are the subjects of this volume. This is what the book tells readers; these are the signs of chemical *dependency* in young people, in contrast with abuse; this person has it; let's get him or her to stop drinking and using other drugs through a successful treatment model, the Minnesota Model as it is specifically applied to young people, not adults.

Essentially, the book deals directly with the continuum of care from intervention to rehabilitation, arguing clearly and concisely that chemical dependency can be diagnosed, that its impact on young people can be assessed, and that young people can be rehabilitated and restored to productive and creative living.

The book then goes on to describe in detail a program that has successfully accomplished just that for the past decade at Hazelden Pioneer House. Readers will be particularly grateful for the sections on psychological testing—especially for the learning disabled, the assessment process, group strategies, planning for aftercare, working with families, and much more.

The authors—my colleagues and friends—are eminently qualified to write this book. They have treated hundreds of chemically dependent young people at Hazelden Pioneer House and have given hope to them and their families. This book is an effort to assist others who want to provide similar help to a population at risk throughout the United States. It is indeed a serious and valuable contribution. Everyone concerned with the problems of alcohol and other drug dependency will be well rewarded for having read it.

Damian McElrath, Ph.D.
Director of Residential Services
Hazelden Foundation
Center City, Minnesota
October 1988

PREFACE

Chemical dependency has touched the lives of thousands of young people and their families. It is a difficult illness to treat, and is made even more complicated by the emotional and developmental issues of the young person. Effective treatment must take into account improving the quality of a young person's interactions with his or her environment, if not changing the environment itself. Many factors play a role in shaping those interactions:

- Family dynamics
- Sociological determinants
- Legal and judicial policies
- Peer relationships
- Psychological determinants
- Educational and school policy issues
- Special needs such as physical or emotional impairment
- Physical health
- Religious beliefs and spiritual needs
- Financial resources

Interpretation of these factors will shape professional responses, including evaluation and diagnosis, treatment plans, and strategies for aftercare and relapse prevention. Such complex interactions may eventually involve the community at large in evaluating prevention philosophies, research and education resources, and public awareness and commitment.

The treatment of chemical dependency in young people is complicated further because professionals in the field do not always agree on the problems, much less the solutions. For example, some treatment professionals believe that most young people who abuse alcohol and other drugs and then display inappropriate behavior should automatically be placed in inpatient treatment programs. Others insist that outpatient programs be tried prior to resorting to inpatient treatment. Still others believe that young people cannot become chemically dependent at all and that their involvement with alcohol and other drugs is only normal rebellion.

Even among those who do accept that chemical dependency is a disease that can be diagnosed in adolescence, there are disagreements. Issues being debated include assessment guidelines, length of stay in treatment or aftercare, and training requirements for health care providers. These disagreements result in part from counselors' diverse educational backgrounds, which produce differing beliefs about treatment approaches.

In addition, external regulating forces such as licensures, staff credential guidelines, and operating policies and procedures are inconsistent among treatment facilities. Some insurance companies also play a role in shaping different approaches by attempting to regulate treatment standards so that, for some facilities, the treatment offered is based more on the insurance company's policies than the patient's needs. Nevertheless, out of all the debate and disagreement about procedures and practices, effective treatment methods have evolved. One such treatment approach, developed in the 1950s, is the Minnesota Model, and many of the theories and practices described in this book come out of the authors' experience with and commitment to that approach.

Our professional and personal commitment to those who suffer from drug dependency has prompted us to formally address the problem of adolescent and young adult chemical addiction. We believe that we can offer important information we've learned from our teachers: the hundreds of chemically dependent young men and women we have treated and their families. Much of our information is based on our interaction with them, along with the knowledge gained through our education and professional training. It has been the young people and their families who have taught us the basic concepts of an individual treatment approach:

- a respect for human dignity,
- the encouragement of self-respect, and
- the recognition of the right of a person to refuse treatment.

These basic principles can produce powerful results, and they are the foundation for our work.

We are deeply indebted to our colleagues who work in treatment programs for adolescents and young adults. We also wish to express our gratitude to our colleagues in counseling, nursing, psychiatry, and medicine. Through their combined efforts and continued study, additional answers and effective strategies will evolve for treating young chemically dependent patients.

None of us has all the answers. Much is yet to be discovered about this problem. We do, however, offer a positive approach in dealing with adolescent and young adult chemical dependency, and we offer a sense of hope in addressing this complex issue. Our solutions, theories, and opinions may not be right for everybody; what is important is that chemically dependent young people receive the most effective treatment and help possible.

CHAPTER ONE

ISSUES IN ADOLESCENT AND YOUNG ADULT CHEMICAL DEPENDENCY

Young people can experience quality lives free from the effects of alcohol and other drugs. They can do so by abstaining from the use of alcohol and other drugs, by committing themselves to the goals of their individual treatment plans, and by committing themselves to living the Twelve Steps of Alcoholics Anonymous. We view the treatment of chemical dependency in adolescent and young adult patients to be moderately successful when the patients involved sincerely want to stop their use of addictive substances.

Terminology

Throughout this book, certain terms will be used in particular and precise ways. We define *adolescence* as the period between the ages of thirteen and eighteen; *young adult* refers to the time between the ages of nineteen and twenty-five. We use the terms *young people* and *young patients* to cover both

1

groups. By *drugs*, we mean alcohol and other mood-altering substances.

Professionals in the field of chemical dependency treatment often use the terms *chemical dependency* and *addiction*, and we do also, though we recognize distinctions between them. We define *chemical dependency* as a physical condition that exists when the body needs alcohol or other drugs to function in a normal manner. As a person's use of alcohol or other drugs increases, the body's tolerance for the drug increases, causing the body to demand more of the drug for normal functioning. *Addiction* implies a compulsive and habitual behavior that usually has negative consequences. *Chemical addiction* is the repeated ingestion of alcohol or other drugs despite the negative consequences of their use.

The term *treatment* covers a variety of possibilities for getting help for chemical dependency. Some of the possibilities open to a person in treatment include individual counseling with a psychologist or psychiatrist, individual or family pastoral counseling, and group counseling led by a professional. Patients can receive this and other types of counseling on an *outpatient* basis. This means that they live at home and continue going to school or work, and attend treatment sessions several times a week for several weeks or months. Alternatively, some patients receive *inpatient* treatment, meaning that they become full-time residents of a treatment facility for a period of time ranging from weeks to months. Treatment possibilities are discussed at length in Chapter Seven.

Unique Dilemma of Chemical Dependency in Young People

To facilitate discussion, we've divided the complex issues that surround adolescent and young adult chemical dependency into three areas. First, adolescent and young adult chemical dependency differs substantially from adult chemical dependency. Second, adolescents and young adults are in the midst of making an enormous physical and psychological transition – that of changing from children to adults. Third, certain social conditions have a great impact on some young people and contribute to their chemical dependency. Each point is discussed below.

Difference between Adults' and Young People's Dependency

Chemical dependency among young people is a different and often more complex problem than chemical dependency in adults. This complexity has several sources: Young people lack adult coping skills, and most have not separated completely from their parents. Moreover, many young people feel sexually insecure and inadequate. They have not yet had meaningful loving, bonding relationships with members of the opposite sex. Also some young people fail to achieve in life's ordinary tasks such as at school or on the job, and consequently never receive recognition from their peers and community.

Because of the complexity of young people's chemical dependency experience, the standard twenty-eight day inpatient treatment model may be ineffective. One reason is it was initially designed for middle-aged adults. Specific treatment strategies for adolescents and young adults will be discussed in later chapters.

Developmental Hurdle of Adolescence

Any approach used in working with young people needs to begin with the premise that adolescents' physical and psychological development is in transition. Too often, professionals overlook or discount this point.

The hormonal changes that occur during adolescence accelerate physical growth and sexual maturation. Adolescents' sexual maturation is attended by an array of social customs, rituals, and beliefs, and by religious prohibitions and behavioral expectations. All of these complicate adolescents' sexual expression. In addition, families typically voice opinions about their children's sexual conduct. The messages that fam-

3

ily, religion, and society give adolescents may account for many of today's adolescents being frightened, insecure, and preoccupied with their possible physical inadequacies.

Young people often feel awkward and insecure in other ways. They frequently feel inadequate about their physical appearance, rate of intellectual maturity, popularity with peers, school achievement, ability to move comfortably in the adult world, and ultimate prospects of functioning as independent adults.

Because adolescence is a time of frustration, it is also a time of anger and rebellion. Young adults want to break away from the control of parents but often cannot because they can't afford to leave their parents' home. For their part, parents are often ambivalent about their adolescent children's desire to move away. On one hand, they want their children to understand that they are loved and wanted at home; on the other, they sense their children's growing rebellion, frustration, and need for freedom. Many occasionally yearn for the day when their children will leave home.

All too often, honest statements of frustration or unhappiness by young people or their parents are followed by feelings of guilt and remorse and by a willingness to give in to the demands of the other. The rise in family tension has led families into counseling in ever-increasing numbers as new programs have emerged to partially meet demands not present one or two generations past.

As will be discussed in Chapter Four, adolescents mature into young adults by completing a series of developmental stages or tasks. Completion of these tasks can be delayed by two or more years when an adolescent is chemically dependent. This means that the chemically dependent adolescent who is seventeen years old may have the social and emotional maturity of a fifteen-year-old.

4

How Social Conditions Influence Young People's Dependency

Adolescent and young adult chemical abuse and dependency are serious worldwide problems that defy simple explanation. It is not enough to say that our young are alienated from the basic societal values (such as strong family ties, religious training, and work ethic) and the sense of belonging that earlier generations held. Though the increasing number of divorces and single-parent families have created economic hardships, this does not explain the increase in alienation. Such hardships sometimes bring families closer and strengthen mature, responsible behavior in young people.

Much has been said and written about the negative consequences of the urbanization of people that has accelerated in the Western world during the past fifty years. To some observers, the shift in population from rural communities to city environments has contributed to a loss of personal identity and to a deterioration in ethical morality among young people. Some believe today's young adults have become self-centered or narcissistic and far too negligent of the needs of others. Such observers see adolescents and young adults as being interested mainly in living their lives in the pursuit of pleasure and material objects.

In addition, young people may be adversely affected by the electronic media, which provide instant news reports, allowing everyone to share in the tragedy and pathos of a suffering world. For middle-aged people, the experience of having instant access to tragedy on a worldwide basis has occupied only a part of their lifetime. Elderly people in this generation have experienced relatively slow and easy changes in communication technology.

Instant communication, however, has always been a part of the lives of young people. At a young age, they are aware of the potential destruction of human life through an atomic holocaust, increasing industrial contamination, or some as-yet-unforeseen disease. Because of this awareness, many young people may view the world from a different perspective than do their parents and grandparents.

In the rest of this chapter, we'll show you why chemical dependency is a spiritual illness, and how poor mental health can affect young people's chemical dependency. We'll also look at our drug-taking society and how it contributes to a young person's physical addiction to chemicals. Then we'll discuss how Twelve Step programs can help the chemically dependent young person recover.

A Spiritual Illness

A lack of spiritual development may contribute to young people's addiction to alcohol and other drugs. In this way, they are similar to adults who are chemically dependent. The following story demonstrates the importance of spiritual development to recovery from addiction—for young people and adults.

In 1961, Bill Wilson, one of the founders of Alcoholics Anonymous, wrote to Swiss psychologist Carl Jung asking him to explain the recovery of Roland H., who had been an alcoholic patient of Jung's in the 1930s. In his letter, Wilson asked what aspect of Roland H.'s recovery Jung thought was the most significant. Jung's response was unequivocal. In Jung's opinion, Roland H. had recovered because he was able to see his thirst for alcohol "as the equivalent, on a low level, of the spiritual thirst for wholeness, expressed in medieval language [as] the union with God."[1]

Jung's letter can be interpreted to mean that he believed a necessary prerequisite to recovery was an acknowledgment by the patient of the inability to deal rationally with the problem, and a willingness to turn the problem over to God in a trusting way. The patient's decision transcends rationalism; it is rooted deeper in the human psyche.

Mental Health: A Complicating Factor

Many chemically dependent young people are in poor mental health. Even if they were not chemically dependent, they would do poorly at home, in school, or in their general environment. These young people cannot tolerate stress, are overly impulsive and angry, and are unaware of others' feelings. They experience wide mood swings, depression, or panic attacks and show symptoms of being out of touch with reality. In a wider context, their personality disorganization is identified as schizophrenia. For these unfortunate young people, chemical dependency is only one more complication in lives that are already intolerable. We will discuss these and other psychological characteristics of chemically dependent young people in Chapter Three.

Physical Health: A Drug-Taking Society

Chemical dependency is the cause of many medical problems. Some experts consider the illness to be the foremost health issue today, particularly given the number of deaths attributable to chemical dependency. This death statistic would be staggering if the fatalities caused by chemical dependency were properly assigned. As it is, they are often labeled automobile fatalities, suicides, and overdoses; this mislabeling keeps the public from recognizing the severity of the problem. Nevertheless, today the media is not mislabeling as much, and there is a wider awareness.

Chemical use has changed in the past twenty-five years. In the 1950s alcohol was the chemical most commonly used by young people. This changed in the 1960s as the United States underwent rapid social change, primarily as a result of the Vietnam War. For many young people, the 1960s and early 1970s were a time of pharmacological discovery. They acted as though there were a pill to fix everything, filling their medicine

7

cabinets with prescribed Valium, taking amphetamines to control weight, and using illegal drugs such as pot and LSD to express rebellion.

Young people in the 1980s have found the means to produce chemicals in makeshift laboratories. Drug counselors and former users report that these synthetic drugs act simultaneously as both stimulant and depressant, and long-term physical and emotional effects are still being observed. As an example, some young people have added the cocaine derivative crack to their more traditional choices of addictive substances such as alcohol and marijuana.

We are a drug-taking society, surrounded by images of people using and abusing chemicals. Television advertisements depict drug use in two ways: Some ads link drug use (drinking) to having fun, for example, while others link drug use (medication) to getting relief; both give the consumer the message that there is a drug to alter every human feeling and mood. At the same time that magazines aimed at young women advertise diet pills that can be bought through the mail, the national news media cover the use and abuse of steroids by young male athletes.

Hundreds of kinds of prescription drugs are available to young people legally and illegally. Moreover, today's youth have learned that they can get high from a proliferation of inhalants such as gas aerosols, glue, paint thinner, and some brands of felt tip markers. The list of chemicals that can be abused appears endless, and the sources are multiplying. It seems likely that the increase in the number of chemicals available will result in a higher risk or potential for chemical dependency and its related problems among tomorrow's adolescents and young adults.

The Physically Addicted Young Person

According to data from the Surgeon General of the United States and from the American Medical Association Task Force on Chemical Abuse, most young people experiment with chemicals before reaching eighteen years of age. Although a multitude of mood-altering drugs is readily available, alcohol remains the chemical of choice for many adolescents.

Chemically dependent young people form only a small fraction of the population who use or abuse chemicals. Most people (young and old alike) who use chemicals do not develop chemical addiction. Many choose to drink or use other drugs only in social settings. These young people seldom find themselves in crises or experience interruptions in their daily living patterns.

Other users, however, develop chemical addiction. They may cause family chaos, drop out of school, get into trouble with the law, alienate themselves from their peers and from society, and contemplate or attempt suicide. Addiction in young people can sometimes result in premature death. It appears there is no single cause to explain why some young people become chemically dependent.

It is always difficult to know which young people are chemical abusers and which are truly addicted. We believe the line of separation for many is very fine. We also believe many young people are referred to treatment programs when the question of their dependency has not been adequately resolved. In our opinion, there are several abusing young people for every one who is truly chemically dependent.

Put another way, there are several abusing young people for every one whose addiction is actually controlled by the brain center's hypothalamus, where true addiction seems to be determined. The biochemical and neurological functions involved in the addictive process are not fully understood as yet. But those working in the chemical dependency treatment field have recognized a significant difference between substance abuse and chemical dependency. In the case of substance abuse the patient's behavior seems still to be mediated in the cerebral cortex of the brain rather than the hypothalamus. The cerebral cortex is the big and new part of the human brain. It mediates such things as memory and cognition. The hypothalmus is the old part of the brain that humans share with other primates. It controls such basic survival needs as thirst, hunger, respiration, and sexuality. True addiction is mediated at this level but abuse is not.

Unlike the abuser, the addict experiences a compulsion to use which is not subject to rational or voluntary control. In many ways the addicted person's compulsion seems to actually resemble the other primary human drives mediated in the hypothalamus like hunger, thirst, sexuality, and breathing. We can, of course, decide to breath or drink, but the processes involved occur without our cognition.

We also believe that addiction is a family or genetic disease, and this concept will be discussed in Chapter Two. Finally, we believe that for the truly addicted person, abstinence from using alcohol and other drugs is necessary for recovery. Alcoholics Anonymous (a self-help organization of alcoholics helping other alcoholics in lifelong recovery from chronic addiction) recognized this about chemically dependent adults more than fifty years ago and about chemically dependent young people more than thirty years ago.

Alcoholics Anonymous and Narcotics Anonymous

Alcoholics Anonymous and Narcotics Anonymous (a self-help group for recovering drug users based on the Twelve Steps of Alcoholics Anonymous) realized as early as 1955 that addicted young people can benefit significantly from following the Twelve Steps. A.A. and N.A. reached that conclusion even though young people's alcoholism and drug dependency is not nearly as advanced or severe as most adult addicts'. The Big Book, *Alcoholics Anonymous*, explains the benefits of A.A. for young addicts this way: "Seeing this danger [uncontrollable drug use], they [young people] came to A.A. They realized that in the end alcoholism could be as mortal as cancer; certainly no sane man would wait for a malignant growth to become fatal before seeking help."[2]

Help for chemically dependent adolescents and young adults is available and we are deeply committed to their treatment. We have seen many restored to family harmony, academic success, and rewarding peer group relationships allowing them to become independent, successful, contributing citizens.

CHAPTER TWO

GENETIC, FAMILY, AND SOCIAL INFLUENCES IN DEPENDENCY

People working in the field of chemical addiction and treatment today commonly accept the axiom that chemical dependency is a family disease. But genetic and social influences also play important roles in the development of dependency. By understanding these influences, professionals are better able to pinpoint causes of dependency in young people and provide effective treatment.

Genetic Influences

Studies of identical twins provide some of the best evidence for genetic influence in the development of addiction. These studies indicate that, generally, when one twin is addicted, the other is also, even when the twins are raised in separate homes or separate families.[1] It has also been well documented that babies born to addictive parents and placed for adoption shortly after birth run a much higher than normal risk of becoming chemically dependent. This appears to be true even if their adoptive parents abstain from addictive substances. The evidence for genetic influence is so conclusive that a well-established history of addiction in biological parents is the greatest single predictor of future addiction in children.

Family Influences

Family characteristics and behavioral patterns related to chemical use are perhaps the second most important influence in chemical abuse and addiction. For example, if family members openly abuse substances, other family members may accept such abuse as normal and approved behavior.

Addiction is always preceded by a period of abuse. The abusive period, the bedrock for the development of addiction, can often be carried out because of some family members' tolerance of chemical use within the family. In such situations, it is common to find several family members in serious and varying levels of addiction. Often, families whose members all abuse alcohol and other substances are bound together in larger kinship units within the same community or geographical area. The substance abuse history of such units is typically long and involves several generations whose substance abuse is a recurring problem for themselves and for the community.

Conversely, some families' prohibitions against using alcohol and other drugs are powerful psychological defense systems or entrenched forms of reacting. For example, in one family a father and two of his sons were terminal chronic alcoholics, while the youngest son was a vigorous crusader against drinking. The youngest son's opposition to alcohol was so extreme that just below the company name and address on his office stationery was printed "Alcohol has many defenders but no defense."

Personality tests have been given both to substance abusers and to those vehemently against substance use. Remarkably, both groups commonly score high on the Minnesota Multi-

Phasic Personality Inventory's MacAndrew Scale and on other tests that measure the presence of an addictive personality.

When members of families that prohibit substance use experiment with substances, they often feel guilty and alienated. Such experimentation is most likely to occur during the stormy period of adolescence when some impulsive acting out and rebellion is normal. Unfortunately, a very complex mixture of anger, fear, guilt, and alienation begins to develop in such families when a family member's substance use is detected. For the person who has been discovered, the road back to family acceptance is likely to be complicated. Few families are truly able to forgive and forget, and a rebellious adolescent spurned by family members is likely to turn from the family and continue substance use with peers and friends. In such power struggles, the rebellious adolescent often places the family second to the peer group.

Social Influences

Advertising and other media messages, as well as churches, schools, the legal system, and other social organizations contribute significantly to young people abusing alcohol and other drugs.

Advertising

Magazine, television, radio, and billboard advertisements for cigarettes, liquor, coffee, over-the-counter remedies, and other mood-altering substances generate revenue for advertiser and media alike. Advertisements help shape consumers' product choices and habits. They encourage consumers to believe that their lives can be enriched by a cigarette, a can of beer, a specific brand of whiskey, an amphetamine such as a diet pill, or a "refreshing" cup of coffee or tea. Often, profit seems more important than concern about the harmful, long-range consequences of using the advertised product. Even when consumers are warned about the possible life-threatening consequences of use, as they are in cigarette advertisements, such warnings seem to be ineffective. Apparently it is easier for many people to enjoy the fantasy of a quiet afternoon spent sailing peacefully in a boat while smoking a cigarette than to heed the more rational warning about consequences like lung cancer and heart disease.

Religion

Virtually every type of mood-altering substance has been thought to enhance the religious experience at some point in history. When such substances were consumed, addiction was seldom a problem because use was specifically controlled and limited to the religious ritual. Moreover, few people would have dared consider abusing a substance that was solely intended to enhance their communion with a diety.

Though few contemporary religions encourage the use of alcoholic or other mood-altering substances, the church still exerts influence on the use and abuse of chemicals. Most world religions including Christianity, Islam, Hinduism, and Buddhism either prohibit or discourage the use of alcohol and other drugs. As a consequence, millions of people who actively participate in a modern religion do not develop addictions because of religious prohibitions. Even those who are genetically vulnerable to addiction do not develop addictions as long as they observe their religion's prohibitions against alcohol and other drug use.

Other Social Organizations

Other social institutions also discourage chemical use and abuse. Health and nutrition organizations scorn the use of alcohol and tobacco. Extracurricular organizations such as state high school athletic leagues have established guidelines prohibiting use of chemicals and tobacco. Groups aimed at providing moral and recreational leadership for youth also frown on the use of alcohol and other mood-altering drugs.

In addition, most countries in the Western world have laws that control the use or abuse of addictive substances and that demarcate legal substances from illegal ones. Through these laws, governments control or monitor the use of some substances such as alcohol, while prohibiting the use of other substances such as heroin and cocaine.

When a country's legal system permits the use of alcohol or other drugs, it also invariably permits the government to raise revenue from the sale of such substances through licensing fees and taxes. By implication at least, the government sanctions the sale and use of such substances through its licensure and fiscal agencies. At the same time, public health and other government agencies attempt to warn consumers of the hazards of such use. The government's position is ambivalent at best – the realities of funding the government appear in opposition to concerns for the health of citizens vulnerable to developing addictions.

In the United States, the legal system has clearly defined rules for tobacco and alcohol use. One must attain a minimum legal age before being permitted to purchase alcohol and tobacco. In addition, well-defined laws prohibit the use of motor vehicles while intoxicated. These laws, however, are not always enforced consistently and often do not provide a sufficiently strong deterrent. The United States may be able to learn much from Scandinavian and Latin American countries, which enact and enforce much stronger penalties for dangerous and abusive chemically-induced behavior. Harsher legal penalties for driving while intoxicated or for transporting or selling illegal drugs are finding a favorable climate in the United States now.

CHAPTER THREE

PSYCHOLOGICAL CHARACTERISTICS AND CONFLICTS

Chemically dependent young people very often have serious underlying mental health problems. It is difficult for professionals to determine which came first, the substance abuse or the mental health conflicts. Regardless, the behavior of typical young addicted people resembles that of young psychiatric patients and young delinquents more than it does the behavior of their nonaddicted peers.

For approximately twenty years, one of the authors, Dr. Dennis Hogenson, has systematically evaluated the personality characteristics of adolescents who abuse and are dependent on chemicals. He has conducted most of his evaluations in a clinical setting where standardized psychological tests are routinely administered. The tests have included objective and projective personality instruments, individual and group tests of general intelligence, and screening surveys for learning disabilities. Objective personality tests include the Minnesota Multi-Phasic Inventory (MMPI) which will be discussed in depth in this chapter (for further information on what MMPI scales measure, see the MMPI manual). The questions and scoring procedures are standardized. Projective personality tests include the Rorschach. The patient is free to associate to the stimulus or task without being confined to specified responses. Dr. Hogenson has also interviewed thousands of patients and examined their histories. Most of the information in this chapter is taken from his extensive clinical experience.

Our discussion will first focus on individual problem areas in the personalities of chemically dependent young people. Then we'll look at the complex personality profiles treatment professionals most often encounter. Lastly, we'll show how young patients with learning disabilities can be best helped in treatment.

Common Personality Traits

Even when the background of a typical chemically dependent young person is unknown, some basic assumptions can be made. First, it is statistically probable that the patient is a cigarette smoker. When a young person has become dependent on chemicals, it is very likely that one of those chemicals will be nicotine or that he or she will be a nicotine abuser at the very least. Dr. William Glasser, the developer of reality therapy—a system of counseling used extensively in treating chemically dependent adolescents—observed the difficulty in giving up cigarette smoking: "If you give a heroin addict the choice of giving up either his heroin or his cigarettes, . . . he would give up his heroin."[1] Nonsmokers are so rare in populations of young chemically dependent patients that faulty diagnosis is suspected when nonsmoking patients appear in treatment programs. Medical conditions such as chronic asthma that prevent a young person from beginning to smoke are obvious exceptions.

The second most common trait in the population of chemically dependent young people is a well-established family history of chemical dependency. Though it is not necessarily true that children of alcoholic parents abuse alcohol, it is frequently true that they abuse one or more addictive substances.

A strong relationship has not been found between chemical dependency and characteristics such as birth order, geographical origin, economic status, or urban versus rural residence. Chemically dependent young people seen in treatment facilities do tend to fit into these categories:

- they are first born,
- East or West Coast residents,
- members of the lower socioeconomic classes, and
- city dwellers.

But it is the large numbers of people found in these categories, rather than the characteristics themselves, that account for the large representation of people with these characteristics in treatment programs. A big share of the chemically dependent population does live in urban areas, but this environment also produces more than its share of other kinds of social problems.

No impressive correlations have been made between the development of addiction and

- age of first use,
- broken versus intact family background,
- intelligence, or
- the occupational status and income of addicted people or their families.

Chemically dependent young people do, however, regularly exhibit specific personality and behavioral characteristics. These characteristics are discussed in the remainder of this chapter.

Delayed Social and Emotional Maturity

Professionals who work with chemically dependent adolescents commonly observe that adolescents stop growing socially from the time their addictive use begins. Data from the

21

MMPI and Rorschach (personality and intelligence) tests indicates that the most consistently occurring personality characteristic in the adolescent and young adult treatment population is a delay of two or more years in social and emotional maturity compared with healthy young people. This developmental delay includes

- potential for abnormal impulsiveness and aggressiveness,
- a limited tolerance for frustration, and
- a poor tolerance for authority figures.

These young patients also seem to be deficient in developing a superego or conscience and to be narcissistic, meeting their own needs at the expense of others. They also consistently lack self-esteem and show little concern for the self-defeating consequences of their behavior.

Moderate and Unstable Mood Swings

Scale nine on the MMPI, which measures hypomanic behavioral characteristics, is frequently above normal in treatment populations. This scale can indicate the possibility of underlying depression, which is complicated by chemical abuse. It is typical for treatment counselors who work with addicted young people to identify large numbers of their patients as depressed. Unlike most adult patients, however, young patients may not look or sound depressed. They frequently act their depression out in a variety of complex ways, such as

- showing extreme moodiness,
- performing less well in school or dropping out entirely,
- shirking responsibilities previously met at home or at a job, and
- showing uncharacteristic delinquent behavior.

Depressed adolescents commonly talk of suicide. Adolescent girls more often talk about suicide, but adolescent boys more frequently carry these threats out. Background data for eighteen adolescent suicides in Minnesota over the past ten years indicate that in all but three cases, chemical abuse or actual dependency was evident.

Alcohol, the most abused substance in the United States, is perhaps the most dangerous substance for people subject to depression and unstable mood swings. Alcohol depresses the central nervous system, and after an initial period of euphoria, a period of depression invariably follows. The depression intensifies with chronic abuse. The stereotype of the happy drunk is the exception rather than the rule. Some depressed people who abuse alcohol become more depressed rather quickly. At such times, suicide can become a genuine concern.

Alcohol abuse often deepens the depression of people who suffer from bipolar depression and makes their manic periods more extreme, heightening their impulsivity and overactivity. They can become extremely hyperactive, verbal, delusional, and often quite grandiose. They often start projects they cannot finish and squander their money as well as that of their family and friends. When these patients begin treatment, they often need to be stabilized with medications such as lithium carbonate before they can respond normally to treatment.

Bipolar depression is just one of several forms of depression which appear to be endogenous, often chronic, and of genetic and biochemical origin. While chemical dependency complicates these depressions, it is not thought to be their cause. Just as lithium is effective with manic-depressives, various antidepressants, when prescribed and used judiciously, have been very helpful to growing numbers of patients diagnosed as depressed. It can be particularly tragic when these people, thinking the cause for their depression lies outside themselves, take drastic measures such as leaving home, school, or jobs with the false hope of finding greater peace of mind.

Chemical Dependency and Impaired Reality Testing

Many of the addictive and psychedelic substances abused by young people distort reality. Such chemicals include LSD, marijuana, hashish, peyote, THC, and PCP. For reasons that are not clear, many patients who abuse psychedelic substances are quite unstable before beginning to use chemicals. Young people in the early stages of schizophrenia and with certain borderline personality disorders in particular seem to abuse psychedelics. Perhaps in the chemical triggering of distorted reality, these people find parallels to their own naturally declining hold on reality. Their drug distorted reality sometimes becomes a normal state for such patients.

Paranoia

The case histories of some patients who abuse substances show that well-defined classic paranoid symptoms appear after the patients' use marijuana. In these cases, patients report that people have been staring at them or talking about them behind their back. Patients who inhale solvents, aerosol sprays, and gasoline fumes also frequently report distorted reality. Permanent organic brain damage is evident in some patients with extensive histories of snorting inhalants.

More Problems

Other symptoms of emotional disturbances have been observed to a lesser extent in chemically dependent young people. These sometimes include either extreme introversion or extroversion, schizoid tendencies, overdependence on others, and a devastating sense of alienation or devaluation of oneself. Some patients have unwarranted fears of physical illness and disease, while others are chronically tense, fearful, and unable to eat or sleep normally.

Sexual Maladaptation

Many chemically dependent adolescent boys reject traditional male values and typical masculine behavioral patterns. Adolescent girls often are so insecure about their maturing sexuality that they grossly overreact by becoming extremely seductive, sexually provocative, and easy prey for both exploitative adolescent boys and men. Evidence indicating that young chemically dependent men and women have had inadequate parent models is abundant. The transition from childhood to adolescence is difficult for many young people. When they adopt chemical abuse as a lifestyle, they reject traditional sex-linked patterns of behavior in order to salvage some sense of individuality.

Complex Personality Profiles

Because the human personality is not commonly uniform or given to fixed definition, treatment professionals usually do not encounter the person who is only depressed, fearful, developmentally delayed, angry, or thought disordered. Patients are more typically very complex mixtures of several personality disorders and conflicts. There are, however, some predictable combinations of personality disorders that are often evident in chemically dependent young people.

A Typical Chemically Dependent Adolescent

This is a boy between the ages of fifteen and eighteen. He is from a family headed by his biological mother and his biological father or a stepfather. He is either the oldest or youngest child. Although this boy has normal intelligence, he is failing in school, and his school principal has probably noticed irresponsible conduct and truancy. He is a cigarette smoker and would be described by others as moody, unpredictable, unreliable, and hard to live with. He causes many family conflicts and frustrations. At least one of his biological parents, biological grandparents, or both has a history of chemical dependency. He has difficulty holding part-time jobs, and he has no realistic plans for the future. At times he may seem somewhat grandiose, overly optimistic, overly energetic, very talkative, and too impulsive about his commitments. At other times he may seem depressed, unhappy, and lethargic. He probably has also come to the attention of the juvenile court system for drug-related offenses, which may have occurred while he was operating a motor vehicle.

Of course all adolescent and young adult patients do not fit this picture, but many do. Young chemically dependent patients seem to behave in certain patterns that can usually be predictably measured by standardized personality tests such as the MMPI where they are likely to display more maladaptive psychopathology than do their nonaddicted peers. Combinations of behavioral traits typically observed in young chemically dependent patients and frequently profiled by the MMPI are discussed in the following section.

Behavioral Patterns Profiled by MMPI

Elevated Scales Two and Four

Elevated MMPI scales two and four have long been considered the bedrock chemical dependency profile. Though this profile does occur in adolescent and young adult patients, it is less commonly seen in young people than in adults. The elevated two and four profile suggests delays in social and emotional maturity, together with impulsive and aggressive tendencies. But unlike the more delinquent and character disordered patient who also has many of these same behavioral tendencies, patients of the elevated two and four profile seem unable to avoid their impulsiveness and overwhelm their personalities. When this occurs, these patients escape into alcohol or other drug abuse, which results in even more depression later in their lives.

Elevated Scales Four and Nine

The combination of elevated scales four and nine on the MMPI shows a patient who is conspicuously delayed in social and emotional maturity. These patients do not seem to have internalized a strong superego or conscience, and they do not appear to be concerned about the consequences of their behavior on their own lives or the lives of others. They are impulsive, aggressive, and delinquent. Because they fail to learn from the negative consequences of their actions, their behavior appears to others as self-defeating. In the short-term, these patients may appear rational, pleasure oriented, and at times extremely caring in their relationships. In the long-term, however, they are not able to maintain friendships because of their irresponsibility and unreliability and their tendency to exploit others. Though such patients seem pleasure oriented, they seldom give reason to believe that they experience any real feelings or emotions. This suggests that a deep core of unconscious depression may lie beneath their surface behavior.

Elevated Scales Two, Four, and Seven

A combination of MMPI scales two, four, and seven describes the typical young patient who may fail to respond successfully to treatment. This profile is usually associated with chronic alcoholism that is secondary to an anxiety psychoneurosis. Patients of this type are subject to borderline chronic depression, are fearful in social relationships, and are chronically tense and fearful about decision making. Though they believe their chronic alcohol consumption enables them to function in life, they fail to understand that alcohol is actually exacerbating their symptoms. Typically, these patients have at least one parent, usually a father, who is tyrannical, domineering, and fear-inducing and who maintains his power in the family through threat and intimidation.

Elevated Scales Four and Eight

The MMPI profile of elevated scales four and eight describes the patient who is developmentally delayed or immature, impulsive, and angry. This patient has a limited tolerance for frustration and for authority figures. As their tolerance declines and the problems in their lives increase, they often become suicidal.

Elevated Scales Two, Seven, and Eight

The most commonly observed MMPI profile in psychiatric populations is the combination of elevated scales two, seven, and eight. Patients of this type are also seen in chemical dependency treatment populations, where they require considerable support, encouragement, and tolerance from their counselors and their peers. These patients show long-term symptoms of emotional conflict that usually prove to be chronic and very difficult to treat successfully. They report feeling depressed, fearful, and unable to cope; they often withdraw from others as their symptoms intensify. Loss of appetite and sleep difficulties are common. Though chemical dependency treatment is often successful, these patients usually remain unhappy, frustrated, and insecure even after treatment.

Some patients in the young adult treatment population are psychotic. These patients usually have significantly elevated MMPI scales often involving scales six, eight, and nine. Their chemical abuse has to some degree masked their acute behavior problems. They are often delusional, paranoid, and cognitively confused, frequently reporting unfair treatment by their family or spouse. It is difficult for these patients to respond in group therapy, and they generally tend to make the treatment staff very uncomfortable. Though these patients can sometimes remain in treatment after receiving appropriate psychotropic medication, they are often best transferred to specialized centers that treat people both chemically dependent and emotionally disturbed.

Validity Scales for Evaluating Young Patients

The MMPI provides four validity scales, which are useful in evaluating young patients. The first validity scale measures only the number of questions the person taking the test ignored or left unanswered. As such, it measures how alert, interested, and responsible the person will be in treatment. To a lesser extent it can also measure visual acuity, reading ability, and the ability of the patient to understand the question well enough to attempt an answer.

The second validity measure is the L, or lie, scale. This scale measures the person's degree of defensiveness and naivete. Statements such as "I do not always tell the truth" can only be answered one way (true). Patients who achieve lie scores of five or higher are often overly defensive and naive in their need to appear better socialized, more mature, and more responsible, than they actually are. When such patients are in treatment, they find it hard to be objective about their past activities.

The third validity scale is the F scale (unlike the L scale above, the F and K scales do not refer to specific terms). The F scale measures the degree of consistency or agreement among the answers a patient gives throughout the test. Patients who have very high F scores fail to read the questions, are very disturbed or retarded, or are poorly socialized or poorly self-disciplined. An elevated F scale is the most frequent cause of invalid MMPI profiles when young patients are tested.

The fourth validity scale is the K scale, which measures the degree to which patients minimize their problems and fake being "good." When a K scale is elevated, all or a part of the score is added to some of the clinical scales to compensate for the behavior of the patient who tends to deny symptoms. In one sense at least, the K scale can be used as a crude measure of self-esteem. While many oversocialized people are defensive and feel a need to deny their symptoms, undersocialized and self-alienated chemically dependent young adults frequently produce low K scale scores. This may indicate their readiness to identify with a troubled life and self-alienation.

29

The MacAndrew Scale

Over the years a number of experimental scales have been developed for the MMPI. One is the MacAndrew scale, which purports to measure addictive tendencies within the personality structure itself. Though the MacAndrew scale does seem to correlate with addiction, it must be used with caution. Many people with very addictive traits have produced low MacAndrew scores (well below twenty), and many nonaddicted people have produced MacAndrew scores above twenty-five.

Learning Disabilities and Chemical Abuse

Psychologists, counselors, and educators have now gained a greater understanding of the damage that an unrecognized learning disability can do to a child or adolescent. Learning disabled children appear to be unintelligent both to themselves and to their peers, regardless of their actual intelligence or creative potential. When failing in reading, life's first organized and institutionally sanctioned task, a young child is usually destined to suffer serious and humiliating damage to an ego that is still overly vulnerable. Children younger than seven and one-half years do not see their problems in a rational, cause-and-effect way. They primarily think in emotional terms. Thus, failure to learn to read means that they are "bad, dumb, stupid," and "not as good" as their classmates. Frequently such children soon develop behavior problems, both in and out of school. Because they are still physically small, however, they can sometimes be managed and controlled in spite of their frustration, unhappiness, and potential anger. But when they become adolescents and young adults, normal adolescent rebellion intensifies, and school and parental contacts no longer provide adequate control. One form their rebellion takes is chemical abuse, which may later escalate into chemical dependency.

Treatment and the Learning Disabled Patient

Learning disabled patients in a chemical dependency treatment program cannot usually be distinguished from their peers by appearance. But it is vitally important to identify them when they are admitted to avoid serious problems in the treatment process. Because these chemically dependent young people have already suffered years of chronic frustration, anger, and diminished self-esteem, they enter treatment with many negative expectations. They do not expect to do well in the treatment process because they have under-achieved and experienced a lot of failure; many have dropped out of school entirely. They believe they cannot read or write very well and, in some cases, have actually done better after leaving school because they have learned to avoid situations where their weaknesses might be exposed.

If patients new to treatment are required to read books and pamphlets and to fill out forms, the threat of exposure for a learning disabled patient becomes very real. Few of these patients are secure enough to admit their limitations to others, and many become defiant. They label the expected academic tasks "dumb" and "boring," and some choose to leave treatment prematurely.

Innovative treatment programs for adolescents and young adults take a different approach. New patients are interviewed orally. They are questioned about their learning problems and about learning problems that their siblings or parents may have. Professional literature advances evidence that learning disorders are genetically inherited and also suggests that approximately six out of seven learning disabled patients are male. Patients are reassured that many famous people – such as scientist and inventor Thomas Edison, actress Whoopie Goldberg, British prime minister Winston Churchill, entertainer Cher, novelist William Faulkner, Arctic explorer Ann Bancroft, and former vice-president Nelson Rockefeller – were also learning disabled. Patients are also assured

31

that they can be intelligent and creative even though they have not achieved well in school. Careful attention is given to convincing patients that their learning problems are understood and that the staff knows how patients feel about reading and writing tasks.

Finally, and of greatest importance, a treatment plan is developed for each patient that emphasizes learning through lecture and conversation rather than from books. The individualized plan allows patients to present reports orally or on tape rather than in writing. Testing for learning disabilities is individual and private so patients will not be embarrassed. Positive testing approaches involve listening to patients read paragraphs of carefully selected materials. Word attack skills, word substitutions, and word omissions are noted. Patients are asked to spell a group of words of increasing difficulty. Spelling is one of the best single screening devices for learning disabilities. Visual decoding is tested by asking patients to find the missing parts in pictures; auditory decoding is checked by asking patients to repeat increasingly difficult lists of letters and numerals.

Upon completion of the diagnostic process, the treatment professional produces a profile of the patient's academic strengths and weaknesses. Strengths are incorporated into the individual treatment plan, and weaknesses are addressed in the daily treatment schedule.

Learning disabilities can represent a significant challenge in the treatment of young patients. And yet, chemically dependent patients with learning disabilities can be treated successfully, and treatment can be one of the most successful experiences in a life previously marked by frustration, anger, disappointment, and self-alienation.

CHAPTER FOUR

ADOLESCENT DEVELOPMENTAL TASKS

Diagnosing chemical dependency in young adults requires comprehensive data collection. To interpret the data correctly, counselors and other treatment personnel must understand the normal adolescent developmental tasks. This makes it possible for them to differentiate normal adolescent rebellion and chemical experimentation from chemical addiction. Treatment plans that fail to incorporate this information are seldom successful.

Levinson's Theory of Early Adult Transition

In discussing later adolescence, Daniel J. Levinson defines the novice stage, ages seventeen to twenty-three, as the *early adult transition stage*. This stage requires two developmental tasks. First, the person must terminate the adolescent life structure by beginning to separate from the parental family. Second, the person must leave the preadult world by discovering a basis for successfully living in the adult world before becoming fully a part of it. Thus, the early adult transition stage

33

allows young people to strengthen their networks of friends and to establish more options and choices for adult living.[1]

The Eight Adolescent Development Tasks

Adolescence can be a time of stress because the environment puts many demands on young people and because young people put pressure on themselves. From age thirteen to age twenty-three, young people need to learn many living skills to grow not only chronologically but also emotionally, spiritually, sexually, and vocationally.

Chemical use and addictive behavior, however, can distort and stagnate the process of adolescent psychological and social growth and keep adolescents from developing living skills.

Barbara M. and Phillip R. Newman expand Erik Erikson's adolescent development stage into eight adolescent developmental tasks. They propose two distinct stages of adolescence—early and late. The early stage includes ages thirteen to eighteen and covers developmental tasks one through four; the late stage includes ages nineteen through twenty-three and covers tasks five through eight.[2] These stages are defined on the following pages.

Understanding normal adolescent growth through a model like these eight developmental tasks can aid counselors and other care providers to more easily evaluate and diagnose addiction. Understanding them will also assist in relating to the tensions and pressures adolescents may experience during these potentially stressful years.

Developmental Task One: Physical Maturation

Adolescents often experience awkward and rapid changes in weight, height, bone structure, and voice. Their sexual organs develop and girls start menstruating. Adolescents often tease each other painfully about these changes. In addition, both teenage boys and girls may be encouraged to dress and act as adults while they secretly wish to hide in a tree house or play with dolls. On the basis of their accelerated physical growth, adolescents are frequently told "You're too old to cry" or "Act your age." Such messages may hurt young people and make them feel confused about their self-image.

Developmental Task Two: Coming to Know Oneself

In the process of coming to know himself or herself, the adolescent moves through complex stages of thinking. This movement is from the concrete to the abstract and involves the use of ever more symbolic visual imagery.[3] In this stage the young adult becomes more reflective and is able to more systematically examine life's problems and possibilities. This can be a time of debates with parents and other authority figures as the young adult develops personal ideas and values.

Developmental Task Three: Peer Group Membership

The adolescent learns and practices social skills outside of parental control by spending more time with friends and less with family members. During this stage the adolescent learns about rejection and acceptance by peer group members and experiences belonging, peer traditions, and group rituals. The adolescent's sense of identity is strengthened by finding a role in a group.

Many conditions—including physical appearance, economic status, drinking behavior and other drug use, and school performance—may determine peer group acceptance or exclusion. Often, adolescents become stereotyped into peer groups such as burnouts, jocks, druggies, brains, nerds, and dropouts. They may find themselves unable to move with ease from one group to another and discover that it is easier to remain where they are than attempt any change in peer group. Or they may become trapped in self-fulfilling prophecies such as "Once a druggie, always a druggie" or "Once a nerd, always a nerd."

Developmental Task Four: Heterosexual Relationships

Adolescents experience increased sexual awareness in male-female relationships. Group dating and other group activities common during the junior high years often change to more exclusive relationships between boys and girls during the senior high years. As adolescents discover a sense of sexual identity, they feel more freedom to experiment with more intimate and often sexual relationships. Sharing feelings, goals, and expectations through "endless" talking and self-revelation is an important activity in the lives of adolescents. Conflicts arise in stormy relationships where drug use inhibits the open and honest expression of thoughts and feelings.

Developmental Task Five: Autonomy from Parents

Independence from family is the primary characteristic in this stage of development. Having a job, a driver's license, a car, and an apartment are typical adolescent goals. In reality, many adolescents are unable to find jobs that provide adequate income, security, and living standards. Thus, they need to rely on their parents to meet the basic needs of food, shelter, clothing, and medical expenses. This can lead to power struggles with parents, school officials, and other authority figures.

Developmental Task Six: Sex Role Identity

This stage requires adolescents to secure their male or female roles and to recognize and practice behavior appropriate to the role. Because contemporary society does not provide clear guidelines for all sexually related behavior, adolescents often have to answer their own questions about the meaning of their sexual role and the possibilities of adult fulfillment within the role. The mass media often portray women as unrealistically romantic and glamorous and men as relentlessly tough and macho, leaving adolescents of both sexes unsure of how to integrate softness and toughness appropriately into

36

their personalities. This may leave them frustrated and confused about when and how to express feelings.

Developmental Task Seven: Internalized Morality

During this stage, adolescents further identify their personal values and beliefs. As they begin to think more abstractly, they develop the flexibility within their thought processes to choose and hold convictions about such concepts as right and wrong, commitment and obligation, and obedience and disobedience. The more interactions adolescents have, the more opportunities they have to choose and commit themselves to personal beliefs. During this stage adolescents may begin to challenge family values.

Developmental Task Eight: Career Choice

A major developmental task for adolescents is making a career choice and planning strategies to ensure their future success. This task can be especially troublesome. It may seem to young people that the adults around them assume the young people are ready to choose with certainty from the wide range of careers available and to begin training for their life's work. Moreover, adults are usually in charge of judging the adequacy of a young person's workplace performance.[4] Because of adult expectations and because young adults' career choices appear so numerous, this period of adolescence can truly be one of confusion and doubt.

In outlining adolescent developmental tasks, it is not the authors' intent to provide conclusive data about the boundaries of these tasks; such a goal would be impossible as human behavior is not totally predictable. What is important is that counselors and professional care providers understand the tasks that confront adolescents. It is paramount that professional treatment personnel be able to evaluate an adolescent's behavior as it reflects the relationship of his or her psychosocial development and use and abuse of chemicals.

CHAPTER FIVE

DETERMINING DEPENDENCY AND ADDICTION IN YOUNG PEOPLE

Successful treatment of chemical dependency in adolescents and young adults relies first on thorough diagnosis of the illness and then on assessment of the young person's needs. Counselors', psychologists', and other qualified professionals' diagnosis of chemical dependency and their comprehensive assessment of the issues surrounding the illness will determine the individual plan to be followed for inpatient treatment and aftercare activities.

Evaluation and Diagnosis of Chemical Dependency

Just as a physician can diagnose a patient's appendicitis, a chemical dependency counselor, along with a team of care specialists, can diagnose the degree to which a young patient is chemically dependent. The team usually consists of counselors, nurses, technicians, chaplains, recreation professionals, and psychiatrists. The difference in the diagnosis is that the physician examines physical symptoms to diagnose appendicitis, whereas the counselor and team examine behavioral symptoms to diagnose chemical dependency. Although many young people do not appear physically ill when they first enter treatment facilities, a thorough evaluation of the behavioral symptoms associated with their drug using patterns is necessary for a confirmed diagnosis of chemical dependency.

Primary Symptoms of Chemical Dependency

Loss of control is a primary symptom of people who are chemically dependent. (See glossary for definition of CHEMICAL DEPENDENCY as distinguished from nondependent chemical abuse or misuse.) Adults and adolescents who only drink or use other drugs socially—that is, they are able to regularly and consistently choose how much they use at a given time and go on to engage in other activities—can be said to have control over their use. Generally speaking, those who drink or use socially and maintain control of their use are not chemically dependent. In contrast, people who are chemically dependent lose control when they drink or use other drugs. Once they start, they continue until they are incapacitated or interrupted. The experience of losing control, plus continuing to use despite the harmful consequences experienced as a result of drinking or using other drugs, defines chemical dependency. The hallmark of chemical dependency, however, is denial. Denial is so built into the disease that it is considered normal for a chemically dependent person to deny the dependency.

Tools such as checklists, questionnaires, and flowcharts help counselors obtain information about loss of control during diagnosis of chemical dependency. The following are those most commonly used methods in determining dependency and addiction in young people.

Heilman's Eight Indicators

Dr. Richard Heilman's eight indicators of chemical dependency are a primary diagnostic tool. Counselors and other team members can use this tool to identify early warning signs, behavioral symptoms, and abusive drinking and other drug using patterns in young people.[1] Heilman's criteria can help the treatment professional evaluate *how* an adolescent uses alcohol or other mind-altering drugs to diagnose chemical dependency in the young person. They are:

- Preoccupation with chemicals
- Rapid ingestion of alcohol and other drugs
- Solitary drinking or other drug use
- Habitual use of alcohol or other drugs for medicinal reasons
- Development of an increased tolerance for alcohol or other drugs
- Blacking out
- Use of alcohol and other drugs without premeditation
- Protection of a private supply of alcohol and other drugs

The counselor needs to consider all eight indicators when evaluating a patient profile for the existence of chemical dependency. Heilman suggests that even the occasional loss of control over the desire to use alcohol and other drugs is symptomatic of chemical dependency. He concludes that if a patient demonstrates four of the indicators on a consistent basis, the patient is indeed chemically dependent and has crossed the imaginary line that prohibits the patient from making logical, clear choices about drinking alcohol or using other mind-altering drugs.

Heilman's Four Characteristics

Heilman also outlined four basic characteristics of innate, compelling human urges that are prevalent in chemically dependent people.[2] The examination of a person for these characteristics is a diagnostic tool that counselors can use to evaluate the presence of chemical dependency.

The first characteristic is the person's recurrent, overwhelming urge "to repeat the experience of 'getting high' or becoming intoxicated."[3] It is beyond the person's will to counteract this urge and refrain from using alcohol or other drugs.

The second characteristic is that the urge to get intoxicated becomes stronger than the need to eat, have sex, or survive.

The third characteristic is that, as the urge to become intoxicated intensifies, it acts independently of any other part of a person's life. This characteristic can arise without requiring outside stimuli such as tension, depression, or excitement; it seeks satisfaction in and of itself.

The fourth characteristic is the state of being psychologically dependent on a drug. This experience is forever etched within a person's mind. It may be reduced with continuing abstinence and occur less often, but as Heilman suggests, it does recur.[4]

Personal Experience Inventory (PEI)

A team of professionals from many clinical and health care backgrounds developed this diagnostic tool. It can be used with children and adolescents between the ages of twelve and eighteen who are being evaluated for problems associated with chemical dependency.[5] The PEI provides information about the severity of the problem related to the young person's chemical use. Specifically, this instrument gives data about the young person's behavior and attitudes and separates the data into the following categories: (1) The extent to which the young person is involved with drugs, (2) the way the young person uses drugs, (3) the way the young person interacts socially, and (4) the existence of any behavioral disorders. The test is easy to administer and can be interpreted by professionally trained clinicians who can determine any invalid responses. In addition to the PEI, a structured diagnostic interview and a short screening test are available for use in preassessments.[6]

Twenty Questions

Johns Hopkins University developed a checklist, "Twenty Questions," which has been revised for use with adolescents.[7] The revised checklist focuses on the young person's behavioral symptoms by asking questions such as

- "Do you lose time from school and work due to using?"
- "Do you crave using at a definite time daily?"
- "Do you use to build up your self-confidence?"

When a patient answers yes to three or more questions, it is a signal to the therapist and other team members who question the young person to pinpoint problem areas that need further exploration.

Jellinek Progression Chart

Developed by Dr. E. M. Jellinek, the Jellinek Progression Chart is used in diagnosing loss of control and chemical dependency. Jellinek separated the progressive nature of chemical dependency into three distinct phases, each with its own specific behavioral characteristics. The Jellinek Progression Chart, a visual tool, outlines the characteristics of each phase.[8]

When a counselor and team identify the behavioral characteristics associated with the *Prodromal Phase*, they can diagnose a patient's alcohol or other drug use as *chemical abuse*. The behavioral characteristics of the Prodromal Phase include increased use of alcohol or other drugs, increased tolerance, hurried ingestion, and preoccupation. During this phase, patients' behavior ranges from drinking or using other drugs occasionally for temporary relief to having periodic memory loss or frequent blackouts as a result of alcohol and other drug use. However, with some drugs such as cocaine, marijuana, and other street drugs, blackouts are uncommon; this limits the usefulness of the Jellinek Chart in diagnosing chemical dependency in young people.

Loss of control is a key indicator in the *Crucial or Basic Phase*, as it is in any diagnostic assessment tool. If the team identifies loss of control and other behavioral characteristics linked to this phase, they can make the diagnosis of *chemical dependency*. Along with the loss of control that accompanies chemical use, the adolescent also experiences other losses – loss of normal living patterns, friends and family, and job, income, and position. Patients may also frequently feel remorseful about excessive drinking or other drug use, guilty about how their behavior affects others, and resentful toward people who live normal, productive lives. In this phase, it is also common for the patient's family to have sent the patient to school, pastoral, or other types of counseling for behavior problems.

When the team identifies the behavioral characteristics of the *Chronic Phase*, they can diagnose *drug addiction*. The key behavioral indicators of the Chronic Phase are continuous use of chemicals, confused thinking, and deterioration of moral values. Physical deterioration is evident by such symptoms as hand tremors and the inability to perform routine tasks.

Assessment of Chemical Dependency

Diagnosis confirms or denies the existence of chemical dependency in a young person; *assessment* examines problems in the young person's life. The diagnosis of the chemical addiction and the assessment of related problems collectively provide a comprehensive patient history. The combination of diagnosis and assessment provide data from which recommendations are made for individual treatment plans and for future aftercare activities.

Assessment is difficult because young patients often deny that they have any problems related to drinking alcohol or using other drugs and are unable to give objective information about their chemical history. It is unusual for adolescents to admit these problems; withholding accurate information about drinking or other drug use is more typical behavior.

44

Denial of inappropriate drinking is discussed in the Big Book of *Alcoholics Anonymous.*

Most of us have been unwilling to admit we were real alcoholics. No person likes to think he is bodily and mentally different from his fellows. Therefore, it is not surprising that our drinking careers have been characterized by countless vain attempts to prove we could drink like other people. The idea that somehow, someday he will control and enjoy his drinking is the great obsession of every abnormal drinker. The persistence of this illusion is astonishing. Many pursue it into the gates of insanity or death. We learned that we had to fully concede to our innermost selves that we were alcoholics. This is the first step in recovery.[9]

Denial renders young patients unable to reveal accurate behavioral data about their drinking or other drug using histories. Consequently, professionals must compile a complete history from people who know the young person. The cooperation and participation of family members is necessary for this process; their knowledge is needed to confirm the accuracy of the information the young person provides. Family support continues to be necessary in the young person's aftercare and recovery.

The open-mindedness of the counselors and evaluators in determining whether a young person is addicted is also essential to the evaluation and assessment process. No diagnosis can be predetermined. No premature assessment about patient needs and treatment can or should be made without a thorough and comprehensive examination of the collected data by a team of professional health care providers.

The assessment of coexisting conditions that affect the patient's life may reveal psychological problems, family problems, eating disorders, or physical problems. Drug history, emotional behavior, physical condition and history, recreational activities, legal status, education and vocational interests, spiritual life, and family history should be included in assessment. Additional pertinent information can be obtained from the person making the referral, which might be a physician, psychologist, probation officer, school counselor, family member, or treatment program alumnus. Each concerned person in the adolescent's life can provide essential information that may answer these basic questions:

- What is this young person's fundamental problem?
- What are this young person's needs?
- Is this person chemically dependent? If so, can this person be treated in this setting?

Chemical History

Perhaps the most important component of data collection is the young person's chemical use. Evaluators need to establish the types and amounts of chemicals ingested and the frequency of chemical use. It is particularly helpful to establish a chronology of the young person's life that reflects major life events as they relate to the person's drinking or drug using history. Evaluations should give special attention to instances when the person lost control and to the consequences the person experienced when using chemicals. The evaluation should record former evaluations and treatments along with the results of any past interventions.

Emotional-Behavioral History

On-site psychological testing using instruments such as the MMPI can reveal the general psychological condition of the young person and predict how well he or she will function in a treatment setting. Information about the patient's emotional and behavioral history should include the patient's history of bouts of depression and suicidal thoughts or attempts related to chemical use. Such information can indicate the level of despondency and the depth of the young person's feelings of guilt and shame because of chemical use.

Counselors should evaluate the person's self-concept and

self-esteem as affected by any conflicts with personal values and beliefs because of chemical use and abuse. As part of the evaluation of self-concept, counselors should determine young people's understanding and beliefs about sexuality and their history of interactions with the opposite sex.

Physical Health

Knowledge of the young person's physical health can reveal limitations such as pregnancy, eating disorders, and undiagnosed illness that might hinder the treatment process. Data about observable scars, cuts, and bruises and information about accidents and falls that occurred while the patient was intoxicated are pertinent to a health history. Information about dangerous behavior such as mixing and injecting chemicals, passing out, blacking out, and overdosing is a vital part of assessment data.

Family History

Information about chemical addiction in a young person's family, including step-family members is relevant to the assessment of the young person. Data about family members in recovery and their involvement with support systems such as Alcoholics Anonymous, Narcotics Anonymous, and Al-Anon is important in gaining a total picture of the family's dynamics. Moreover, awareness of the family system helps predict whether the family will support the young person in the moves from treatment, to aftercare, to long-term recovery.

Educational and Vocational Information

The patient profile is affected by the extent to which the young person likes school, is attending and earning credits or whether he or she is regularly tardy, skipping, or otherwise truant. If the latter behavior is frequently true, it's important to determine if the adolescent is frustrated with school and uses drugs like pot or alcohol to cope with problems. Many adolescents and young adults are school failures and dropouts because of chemical use and abuse, not because of lack of intellectual ability.

Assessment is needed to determine the young patient's specific learning behavior and examine the possibility that a learning disability in reading or writing exists. Tests of general intelligence and reading ability given by psychologists or other trained personnel, can assess the exact condition and level of intellectual functioning. If a learning disability exists, counselors and evaluators should use alternate methods of obtaining diagnostic and assessment information. For example, evaluators can ask patients to draw pictures of their use and to pinpoint their chemical experiences on the Jellinek Progression Chart. The use of colored markers along with music to enhance imagery is another technique which can add creative dimensions to the data collection process for adolescents who otherwise might exhibit denial, resistance, and short attention spans.

Data about the young person's job and other work habits can reveal characteristics typical of using behavior. It's also important for counselors and evaluators to get information about the person's possible employment opportunities following treatment and aftercare.

Recreational Activities and Social Life

It is important to include information in assessment data about how young people spend their leisure time and what their hobbies and interests are. Young people often fail to maintain their interests in team sports, clubs and organizations, and hobbies and crafts once chemicals become an important part of their lives. They often limit their friendships to others whose primary social activities are parties and "keggers" where drugs are available and frequently used.

Legal Status

Many young people enter the treatment process as a result of court intervention. Forced evaluation and eventual treatment can be a negative experience for the patient. Knowledge about a young person's legal status and information regarding pending court dates assist counselors in making an assessment.

Information about a young person's experiences with the law, such as with vandalism, being a run-away, drug possession, and driving-while-intoxicated charges, also influences the assessment interpretation. Use of the Jellinek Progression Chart can help characterize a young person's use and abuse in relationship to the law.

Spiritual Life

Collecting information about a young person's spiritual life is also relevant for a comprehensive assessment of chemical dependency. Young people's former spiritual instruction often conflicts with their current drinking and using behavior. Assessment can determine if chemical use has kept a young person from religious practices formerly engaged in. It's important for counselors planning treatment activities to know if the young person wants to participate in religious practices.

Financial Status

The young person's financial data contribute to the overall assessment profile. Information about the amount and the source of income, along with knowledge about the young person's spending patterns, financial obligations, debts, and savings helps complete the profile of the young person.

Conclusion

Successful evaluation, assessment, and treatment of chemical dependency in adolescents and young adults does not focus on determining *why* the condition exists, but on ascertaining the *exact nature* of the young person's behavior as it relates to chemical use. Chemical experimentation, chemical abuse, and chemical dependency may look similar in any young person entering a treatment facility. But by employing diagnostic tools and comprehensive assessment criteria, along with an understanding of the psychosocial development of young people, a team of professional care providers can successfully evaluate an addictive condition. This evaluation along with information gathered from parent and patient, will allow the team to put into action successful treatment plans.

CHAPTER SIX

REALITY THERAPY IN THE TREATMENT OF ADDICTION

Reality therapy is a system of counseling developed by Dr. William Glasser. Glasser describes its techniques, along with the theoretical basis for its development, in his book, *Reality Therapy.* After hundreds of hours counseling clients using the clinical trial and error approach, and after collectively taking dozens of academic courses and workshops, we have found the principles of reality therapy, outlined below, to be particularly suitable in treating addiction to alcohol and other drugs. More specifically, in our experience, reality therapy best meets the needs of treatment professionals working with chemically dependent young people.

Unlike most other systems of counseling, reality therapy can be learned and effectively practiced by almost anyone willing to apply its principles in a specific and systematic sequence. For reality therapy to work well, however, the practitioner must follow the steps in the counseling sequence in their *exact order.*

Great therapists like Sigmund Freud, Carl Jung, Albert Ellis, Fritz Pearls, and Rudolf Dreikers would probably have been successful regardless of their system of therapy. Their insights and personality strengths would have sufficed in helping their clients understand their problems and become better adjusted. In contrast, most counselors and clinicians need a practical model with a systematic approach, such as reality therapy provides, to deal with the more immediate and concrete issues faced by young alcoholics and drug addicts during a relatively short and intense treatment program.

Reality Therapy Contrasted with Other Forms of Therapy

You can understand the foundations of reality therapy better by contrasting its basic assumptions with those of other forms of psychotherapy. Unlike the *psychoanalytic approaches* of Jung and Freud, reality therapy does not focus on issues in the client's past. Such issues are important, interesting, and sometimes helpful to examine. But it can take a great deal of time for clients to understand their relevance to the counseling process, especially how they apply directly to solving current problems. Reality therapy relegates early life experiences to the unknown, and leaves the matter there.

The techniques of reality therapy also differ from these therapeutic approaches that help clients feel more physically comfortable. In reality therapy, little attention is paid to analyzing or changing body responses such as breathing patterns, muscle tension states, posture, or diet. Reality therapy counselors generally do not use yoga, primal screams, gestalt exercises, massage, or meditation in their practice. These and similar techniques might help people become more content or relaxed but seem to do little to solve practical problems which demand more immediate answers, problems which are typical of adolescent clients in crisis. The direct goal of reality therapy is not to help the client become more content; it is to help the client become more productive and successful.

Rational approaches to therapy, such as the Rational Emotive Therapy of Albert Ellis, focus on sorting the client's thoughts and ideas to correct irrational assumptions on which the client acts in daily life. Therapeutic approaches of this type assert that behavior changes when thinking changes. The observations of reality therapists do not always bear out this connection between behavior and thinking. In spite of this, reality therapy is often closely aligned with the work of Ellis and other rational therapists because of their common focus on finding practical solutions in the present.

The animal research of B. F. Skinner has been applied to *behavioral approaches* to counseling and psychotherapy with varying degrees of success. In general, most reality therapists would agree that it is helpful to analyze present behavior, and then to plan necessary steps for change. Most reality therapists also endorse rewarding instrumental or positive behavior, and extinguishing harmful or unnecessary behavior. People, however, are much more complex than animals, and it is often difficult to maintain predictable schedules of reinforcement outside the laboratory. It has been our experience that patients treated exclusively with traditional behavioral therapy techniques tend to return to their self-defeating behavior after rewards and controls are discontinued.

Changes in Human Behavior: The Background for Reality Therapy

The following is our understanding of Glasser's approach to therapy as it has evolved from his ideas on human needs and social behavior.

Prior to 1950, when young people considered higher education or a career, their primary goal was to earn enough money for their basic needs. Some people also wanted to be able to afford some of the luxuries of life, but it was *only* after first meeting these basic needs for food, shelter, and clothing that other and more exotic goals could be entertained.

53

Many young adults began to take survival needs for granted shortly after 1950. One reason for this change was the sudden abundance following World War II. Other events, such as growing awareness of the threat of thermonuclear holocaust and the increasing influence of mass media, especially television, also had an impact.

For many families this change in values created intense differences of opinion between parents and children. Parents who still believed their children should be prepared to earn money to support themselves as adults were countered by children who took these needs for granted. Young people seemed more interested in pursuing the less tangible goals of personal fulfillment, happiness, adventure, and romance. For Glasser this represented a fundamental change in human motivation and he drew on it heavily in developing reality therapy.

It is Glasser's belief that even when survival needs are satisfied, people still feel unrest and tension, which he termed *pain*. He also believed all people seek to avoid pain and to achieve success. Some people, however, such as those in treatment programs for chemical dependency, have not learned to become successful adults. Instead, they travel a long path ending in addiction. According to Glasser, the steps in that path are as identifiable as the steps necessary for a successful recovery and establishing a new identity.

Where Addiction Begins

As young people grow up, they are likely to feel stress, tension, and pain, even when their survival needs have been met. People have different tolerances for pain. The ability to deal with stress and pain seems to be related to the person's environmental influences and genetic factors, and how realistic their expectation is for a better future.

When young people feel more pain than they wish to or believe they can tolerate, they may find relief by giving up responsibilities which they perceive to be the source of their stress. If continuing to give up responsibilities they believe they can no longer handle almost always results in a sense of relief, along with reduced stress and pain, in a short time, the tendency to give up may become habitual. Sooner or later these young people resemble sinking ships with no surplus cargo to throw overboard; they have nothing left to give up.

Young people in pain with nothing left to give up often express this pain pathologically through physical illness, character disorders, and impulsive, self-defeating behavior. These young people, now sick and often in a physician's care, are no longer expected to achieve normal successes in their lives. Consequently, they may temporarily be excused from being responsible which briefly reduces their pain. When this pain takes the form of chronic neurosis or even psychosis, the patient may earn an excuse from responsibility that can last a lifetime. Similarly, young people who get into trouble because of their impulsive or delinquent tendencies are also excused from responsibility, at least temporarily, which may be further reinforced by time spent in court or jails.

Unfortunately for these people, a time eventually comes when others tire of hearing about their pain and excusing them from responsibility. At this point many of them are likely to take a more drastic step to avoid pain: they move from relating in terms of their pathological symptoms into becoming addicted. As long as addicted people can maintain an abundant supply of their drug of choice, they can continue to avoid pain, and actually believe their lives are fairly pleasurable. If one retraces the long, complex route from addiction to the point where an addict first began to escape from responsibility, one can understand why successful treatment of addiction is such a long and difficult process.

Pathways to a Success Identity

To Glasser becoming successful requires the discovery of *helpful pathways*. In general, these pathways are relatively few and are quite easily defined. Mastery of the pathways to a success identity requires courage, conviction, and determination. If addicted young people are to grow, they can expect to face considerable frustration and discouragement; nature seems to require that people experience some pain to stir them out of lethargy and complacency and on to greater successes.

Giving and Receiving Love

The first pathway to a success identity requires the person to learn to give and to receive love. This may seem superficial to those who have learned to do this as a natural part of their development. Millions of people, however, didn't grow up in environments where family members shared loving feelings. Unless parents can give and receive love, it seems unlikely they will be able to teach those skills to their children.

By using reality therapy, counselors often can help young people become more loving and nurturing toward others and themselves. Becoming more self-accepting and self-appreciating means hard work and may begin with learning to express acceptance, appreciation, and love for another.

Frequently, it is possible to teach young people to become more loving by encouraging them to buy a pet such as a puppy or a kitten. It is less threatening for some people to show love to an animal than to show love to another person, which may seem unnatural and carry the risk of rejection.

Eventually young people need to learn to express love to another person and may need the help of a skilled counselor. A counselor can teach how to give and receive love by guiding the young person through a sequence of progressively more difficult experiences. This may begin with the young person learning to make a simple positive statement about another person's attire or appearance. When expressing compliments becomes easier, the young person can be taught how to make short statements of appreciation for another person's behavior. The last and most difficult part of the teaching experience will be helping the young person learn to comfortably identify and express feelings of warmth, appreciation, and caring for another person. When this is possible, the young person has made a major step toward creating a success identity.

Developing a Skill or Talent

A second pathway to success identity is mastering a skill or talent that the person values and that peers recognize. Some people have a natural talent from birth. Others attain mastery by hours of practicing and perfecting a desired skill. Whether through creative expression, a sport or hobby, academic or vocational excellence, or the acknowledgment and appreciation of a personality attribute, it is concrete experience of genuine recognition that improves self-worth. With such attainment comes a feeling of appreciation for one's importance in the world.

Having Fun

The third pathway to a success identity involves something many people take for granted–having fun. For Glasser, learning to have fun is tremendously important. A spontaneous sense of appropriate humor and the ability to see the lighter side of life is a gift and seems to come naturally to some people.

Unfortunately, there are many people who do not appear to have much room for fun in their lives. When asked when they last had fun, too many people can't remember a single time when they were truly happy.

More than a by-product of living, having fun is essential for true maturation. It is medicine for the psyche and nourishment for the soul. Like learning to be more loving, people can learn to be open to happiness and fun. Whether through recreational activities, travel and adventure, or quietly enjoying the natural beauty of the wilderness, or just going to a movie with friends, it is being open to the possibility for joy in life that's important. This means devoting time, energy, and resources to having fun just as you would to accomplishing other goals in your life.

This process seems to polish rough edges off of living and to put serious or tragic events in a more tolerable perspective. Perhaps balanced living is as simple as working hard, developing our talents to the best of our abilities, maintaining ethical or spiritual integrity, appreciating the beauty around us, developing a sense of humor, and having fun.

Experiencing Freedom

The final pathway to a success identity involves experiencing a sense of personal freedom. Total freedom is impossible but everyone needs to experience some degree of freedom in their lives to feel worthwhile, some more than others. People who are successful and happy are more likely to have more control of their decisions, commitments, and responsibilities. When people permit the expectations of others to control their activities, they usually fail to achieve success and mastery of their lives. The more complicated and time consuming our responsibilities become, the less likely it is that we will maintain autonomy and freedom. Conversely, the more freedom and choice we feel we have, the less threatening the world appears, and the less dependent we are likely to become. Remaining free often involves making sacrifices and requires us to be vigilant and to think critically so we don't lose ourselves completely to the things, people, and events in our lives.

Putting Reality Therapy to Work in Five Stages

Reality therapy, as Glasser describes it, involves specific stages that must be followed in sequence if the healing process is to work.

When the counselor first leads the client through these stages, the process may seem too easy, unsophisticated, or superficial. But counselors who continue to practice it discover its complexities. Even so, counselors can become excellent practitioners fairly early on when they adhere to its basic principles and follow the stages in sequence.

The First Stage: Establishing Friendship

The first stage requires the counselor to make friends with the client. This approach differs from the cold, clinical detachment many therapists employ. Accomplishing the first stage can require only the time it takes to give a warm smile, a friendly handshake, or a few words of sincere welcome. It can take several clinical sessions to actually earn the friendship and trust of a guarded, frightened, or reluctant young person. But it is difficult to begin reality therapy until an atmosphere of warmth and friendship exists, and it is never possible to continue until a trusting and caring relationship is established between the counselor and the client.

The Second Stage: The Problem and What's Being Done about It

The first part of the second stage requires the client – not the counselor – to describe the problem clearly. The counselor can, of course, ask questions to help clarify the problem. But for reality therapy to be effective clients must describe their problem or problems.

The second part of the second stage requires the counselor to ask the client, "What are you doing now to solve this problem?" It is important that the counselor help the client carefully think through the problem and that the client clearly state what he or she is doing to make things better. After hesitating, rationalizing, blaming, and feeling self-pity, the client usually replies, "Nothing."

The Third Stage: Making a Plan

The third stage requires patience from the counselor as the client develops a plan to solve the problem. The client must originate the plan, but the counselor can help by asking clarifying questions. The plan should be practical and achievable, and the client must recognize the plan as his or her own. The

59

client's ownership of the plan is critical because it provides the client with the impetus to proceed to the next stage.

The Fourth Stage: Taking Action

The fourth stage requires the client to make a commitment to put the plan into action. The counselor often encourages this by asking the client questions such as

- "Where can you do this?"
- "How do you plan to do this?"
- "When exactly will you put this plan into action?"
- "Will you contact me first thing tomorrow and tell me how it worked?"

Questions of this type are intended to get the client to *commit to action* at a specific time and place. The commitment is further sealed when the patient agrees to report the results to the counselor.

If the plan works, the counselor can shift the direction of therapy to other problems in the young person's life. But if the plan doesn't work, and it often doesn't, a new plan and a new commitment must be obtained. In developing a new plan, the client must be helped to evaluate the old one to gain an understanding of what is worth repeating and what was ineffective. The counselor must encourage any movement the client makes toward taking action and responsibility. Often a client will need to develop several plans to see a problem through to its logical conclusion.

As young people suffer through frustrations and disappointments, it is important not to punish them further with unwarranted criticisms of their behavior. Our experience shows unwarranted criticism and punishment *never* help anyone.

Just as clients must not be punished, so too the natural consequences of their behavior must not be interfered with. Whenever clients are rescued, excused, or enabled, they are harmed. When natural consequences are obstructed, a patient's growth and development is deterred. An important general rule of reality therapy is *never punish and never interfere with natural consequences.*

The Fifth Stage: Never Give Up

The fifth and final stage of reality therapy asks that the counselor *never give up.* It demands the counselor's total dedication and commitment. Some clients require months and even years of involvement. They need reassurance, support, and friendship when things are not going well in their lives. Most difficult clients provide counselors with many opportunities to give up on them. Counselors must resist this pitfall and remain diligent and persevering. The demands of practicing reality therapy are considerable. Nonetheless, we believe the rewards can be tremendous, both for counselors who practice it and for young people who benefit from its principles.

The two case histories below are presented to give you a better understanding of how these principles work.

Case History Number One: "My father is a hateful person."

Counselor: It's nice to see you Robert. How can I be of help?

Patient: The problem is my father – he's a real jerk. In fact, he's just hateful. I can't stand to be around him.

Counselor: You're finding it hard to relate to your father – to communicate with him?

Patient: That's putting it mildly. I can't stand him. Everything I ask for, he refuses. He won't give me the time of day anymore!

Counselor: What are you doing to make the situation better – to solve your problem?

Patient: I don't understand what you mean. My father is the problem – he's making my life miserable!

Counselor: I understand your point of view, but what are *you* doing to solve the problem?

61

Patient: Well . . . I don't know what to do. That's why I'm talking to you. What should I do?

Counselor: What I mean is, what have you done to improve your relationship with your father, to make things better?

Patient: I don't know what to do. Nothing I've done has worked.

Counselor: What do you want from your father?

Patient: I need money. My rent and car insurance are due, and I'm broke. All my father says is that I should get a second job because it's not his problem.

Counselor: Are there any conditions under which your father would give you a loan?

Patient: I don't think so . . . maybe if I get a second job.

Counselor: How could you best approach your father to find out?

Patient: I suppose by keeping my cool when I call him. Maybe by saying I only want a loan, and I will take a second job to pay him back.

Counselor: That sounds like a good plan. When will you call your father?

Patient: I suppose I could call him at home tonight.

Counselor: Sounds good. Will you let me know tomorrow morning how things worked out?

Patient: OK.

Case History Number Two: "I might start using drugs again when I finish treatment."

Counselor: Hello Betty, you're looking good today. How is your treatment plan coming along?

Patient: It's going good, but I'm worried that when I go back home my boyfriend will want me to use drugs with him again. He's still using, he parties a lot, and I know that sooner or later he'll expect me to use too.

Counselor: He must mean a lot to you if you're willing to keep seeing him under these conditions.

Patient: Yes, I really love him, and in almost every other way he treats me just great. I can't stand the idea of leaving him.

Counselor: I suppose you've already discussed this with your peers and others here on the treatment unit?

Patient: Sure, but they all think I should drop him and find a new boyfriend.

Counselor: And you won't do that?

Patient: No. I love him too much. I won't give him up.

Counselor: What have *you* done to solve your problem?

Patient: I don't know what to do.

Counselor: What could you try?

Patient: Well, I've thought about writing him a long letter explaining to him why I *never* want to use drugs again – to put my reasons for not using in writing so that he can really look them over. I've also thought about asking him to put it in writing that he will never pressure me to use again. You know – kind of like a contract or written agreement.

Counselor: That sounds good to me. When can you write to him?

Patient: Tonight.

Counselor: Do you trust me enough to let me read your letter before you send it, and will you mail it tomorrow?

Patient: Yes.

CHAPTER SEVEN

FUNDAMENTALS OF TREATMENT

Basic Philosophy

Quality chemical dependency treatment programs for adolescents and young adults have a clearly defined philosophy, along with clearly delineated policies, procedures, and standards, to ensure consistent, high-quality patient care. The fundamentals discussed here are based on the assumption that chemical dependency treatment for young people must differ in approach and philosophy from treatment for adults. Three key differentiating factors important to recognize are

- the even greater power peers have in a young person's recovery,
- the young person's higher energy level, and
- the necessity for being even more sensitive to treating young people with dignity and respect.

Peer Power

As young people enter adolescence, family influence decreases and peer influence increases. Consequently, the likelihood that adolescents will make lifestyle changes often depends on whether their peer group will accept and support such changes. Treatment programs can acknowledge this normal and powerful influence by developing peer-based recovery programs. These programs give adolescent patients responsibility for some of the daily functioning of individual treatment plans and for interacting in ways that further each others' treatment outcomes. When the peer-based philosophy is used, peers replace adults as authority figures, at least in part. Moreover, the peer-based approach gives young patients useful guidelines for making positive, healthy choices about their lifestyles.

High Energy

Successful treatment programs also acknowledge young people's high energy levels, along with their uninhibited openness and frankness. Moreover, successful programs discover ways to incorporate this energy into program activities and draw on it to teach an improved lifestyle.

Chemically dependent young people are often chronically bored. They need to engage in recreational activities to replace the time they spent using chemicals. Both indoor and outdoor settings should make creative use of the patients' energy and openness.

An optimum treatment setting will include an outdoor area with walking paths, playing fields, and courts for sports like volleyball and tennis. The placement of benches and tables outdoors encourages picnics and conversation. If possible, the treatment facility's indoor area should have large, open spaces and big windows to give a sense of openness and peace. A spacious game room with comfortable furniture encourages young people to engage in games and activities which involve interaction and intellectual challenge. If a treatment program cannot supply such accommodations, it can make use of community-based facilities, such as picnic grounds and parks, to supply recreational outlets for patients. No matter how limited the accommodations are, the treatment program must help young people channel their energy into creative and rewarding recreational activities. These activities can become alternatives to the boredom which fosters drug use as young people begin a life of chemical abstinence.

Dignity

A successful program for young people ensures that each patient and family member will always be treated with dignity and respect by every employee. The dignity and respect accorded the patient encourages growth and the expectation of successful treatment.

Policies and Procedures

The treatment program philosophy needs to be agreed on and operating before program guidelines can be developed. Daily program guidelines are developed from the program's philosophy, not vice versa.

Policies, procedures, and standards are the nuts and bolts of a treatment program. Guided by the philosophy and implemented by the staff, policies ensure quality patient care. Program policies can define prescreening and admission criteria essential for appropriate patient placement. Procedures can be outlined for maintaining medical records such as doctors' and psychologists' reports and data. Policies and standards can assist the staff in documenting interactions with patients, parents, and other staff members.

Staff Training and Facility Accreditation

Policies can be written to encourage the staff to consult and interact with personnel from other treatment providers. They can specify that staff take advantage of ongoing inservice instruction available in the program and out in the community.

Policies and procedures can also be written to cover accreditation of the treatment facility. State and federal guidelines usually regulate training and accreditation; consequently, a discussion of these topics is beyond the scope of this text. Readers should consult local and state statutes for licensure and facility accreditation information.

Individual treatment programs for young people may set their own standards for staff competency. Programs are most credible to young people, their parents, and the community when treatment centers set high standards while meeting state and federal guidelines.

Treatment policies can set the tone for communication between personnel and patients and their families. The staff needs adequate time to interact with each other and with patients in order to maintain professional standards. To ensure this, policies can be written that mandate time for daily staff meetings; these allow team members to get reinforcement from each other. These daily staff meetings provide patients with a model of teamwork and positive communication. Patients can see that a treatment program consists of action, teamwork, and quality standards. Similarly, their recovery requires action, reliance on others, and practice of recovery principles.

Reality Therapy's Four Positive Beliefs

Treatment philosophies and policies are ineffective if staff and patients fail to communicate positive beliefs. If a program does not define and adopt positive beliefs as the basis from which all professionals work, unhealthy beliefs and attitudes may abound. A program's beliefs should communicate to young people that they are responsible for their own recovery. Reality therapy contains four positive beliefs that have proved successful with young people. These are: you are capable; you can succeed; I believe in you; and we won't quit.

You Are Capable

This belief places responsibility for recovery on the young person. It assumes the staff will give the patient knowledge and skills needed for recovery, and suggests the patient must follow through with daily tasks and treatment plan goals. Thus, the recovering person becomes self-directed rather than staff-directed. The patient assumes the proactive attitude of "I want to do this for myself," rather than the reactive one of responding to a counselor's message of "I told you to do it, now do it!" Additionally, the treatment staff shows respect for the patients by encouraging them to believe they are capable.

A common counseling philosophy holds that, if pointed in the right direction, people can find answers within themselves. By encouraging this process in treatment, health care professionals allow patients to make mistakes and to begin to learn the consequences of their mistakes. As a result, counselors often find patients are more open to suggestions about how to behave less destructively and impulsively.

The peer group is an important component at this point. Some of the patient's peers have already set guidelines for appropriate behavior in treatment. The atmosphere of dignity and respect, along with peer pressure, helps the patient begin to believe the message, "I am capable." In many cases, peers can modify and redirect a patient's attitudes and behavior more effectively than a counselor can in one-to-one sessions.

You Can Succeed

Many young people who enter treatment programs have failed in school, in sports, and in peer and family relationships. Because they have already experienced so much failure, it is imperative that success be built into the treatment program. Success helps the young person feel a sense of accomplishment on which hope and confidence can be built.

A treatment program can help young people develop a sense of success and achievement by recognizing their accomplishments. For example, time can be set aside at peer group meetings to announce names of patients who have completed Twelve Step work. Graduation ceremonies, to which peers, family, and staff are invited, can be held to award medallions that commemorate patients' achievement. Patients can also be recognized for completing treatment plans and objectives. In addition, they can record their positive accomplishments on weekly goal sheets, which can be presented to peers during the peer group meeting. This allows patients to monitor their progress and provides a way for peers to recognize accomplishments and give feedback to each other. These activities and others like them help send the patient the message, "You can succeed."

I Believe In You

This belief recognizes the uniqueness of each patient. With this belief in mind, the staff develops individual goals for patients. The patient's specific talents and skills are recognized during the assessment process, and upon entering treatment, these qualities are incorporated into the treatment plan. When identifying a patient's individuality, the staff considers every detail. For example, a patient's interest and talent in writing poetry or playing music can be incorporated into therapy. Because some patients come from metropolitan areas while others come from rural settings, geography can contribute to a patient's sense of uniqueness. In addition, the statement "I believe in you" means that the staff accepts patients at the patients' level of development; patients don't have to be at the staff's level to find acceptance. The patient-centered approach is the treatment staff's way of affirming the young patient.

We Won't Quit

Reality therapy allows the treatment plan to be changed when an approach doesn't work or when a goal doesn't fit. Individual planning is critical. Some patients have failed so many times that the successes have to be built in within their treatment plan before they can achieve additional progress. Some patients, it seems, set themselves up to fail simply because they cannot consciously conceive of themselves as successful.

This is one of the most difficult and challenging type of patients for counselors and staff to work with. When working with unmotivated, underachieving young people, the treatment team should interact with each other and give each other recommendations, modifications, and support. First, however, the team should discuss a patient's status, brainstorming about strategies that may be helpful. For example, the patient's self-esteem may be heightened if the patient participates in some form of peer government. In addition, some patients feel supported by their peers when given honest, observable feedback about positive qualities and negative behavior. Patients often can see their lack of recovery through peer interpretation and feedback.

The unsuccessful patient may get support during one-to-one counseling sessions with a chaplain or in family sessions with a counselor. The patient can also get support from further testing of academic skills and additional psychological evaluations. Assessment of other medical or emotional conditions may lead the staff to recommend that the patient, after completing treatment for chemical dependency, get treatment in a different setting, where secondary issues can be confronted and addressed.

Additional evaluation may reveal that inpatient chemical dependency treatment is not appropriate for the young person. A wide spectrum of treatment modalities, ranging from a short-term outpatient setting to long-term inpatient facilities, is available to young people. Another option is that the patient, the family, and the treatment team may conclude the patient should try to maintain sobriety in his or her own way. The treatment team can support this decision by establishing a plan with personal goals to be achieved at home.

The staff's message to the young patient is clear: "We won't quit. We're not giving up on you, even though you may be quitting on yourself. We'll be excited about your recovery for you until you are able to be excited yourself."

Conflict Resolution

This is an integral part of the We Won't Quit philosophy. Conflict resolution is a communication process the treatment staff uses with a patient whose progress does not meet the treatment plan's goals, the patient's capabilities, or the treatment unit's expectations. Young people in treatment make mistakes: they may break rules, act inappropriately, and behave negatively. Conflict resolution may help correct negative behavior and prevent a patient's premature dismissal from the program.

As the following example shows, the key to conflict resolution is getting the patient to assume responsibility for negative behavior.

Kyle, a young patient in treatment, has spent several hours contemplating the First Step of the A.A. Twelve Step program. Ready to share his thoughts, Kyle explains to his peers that he is "powerless over alcohol" and that his life "had become unmanageable." The group turns down Kyle's presentation because he failed to give specific examples of powerlessness and minimized his use. Rejected again, Kyle is overcome by uncontrolled anger. Not having any coping skills to help him deal with his feelings, he hits a closet door, puts a hole in it, and bruises his hand.

This relatively common chain of events could have these consequences: Kyle could be discharged from the program as incorrigible, or he could be separated from his peers in a time-out room. Both of these could be unproductive and alienate Kyle from his peers, the staff, and possible help.

In contrast, conflict resolution offers positive outcomes and long-lasting rewards for all concerned. In conflict resolution, the treatment staff's goal is to have Kyle assume responsibility for damaging the door. He can take responsibility by talking to the maintenance personnel, learning the cost of a new door, and paying for it. Most often young people in this kind of situation will choose to accept responsibility for their actions. In some instances, however, a young person's reply might be, "My father will send a check for it." The patient can then be told, "Your father didn't damage the door. You did, and you need to accept responsibility for it."

Typically, Kyle would also be asked to make an appointment with a counselor to discuss his anger, what he does when he is angry, and what he could do differently. The counselor might tell Kyle, "You don't have to punch doors. There are other things to do when angry." Kyle might learn how hurt feelings lead to anger, and how anger leads to resentment. He might also learn that feeling angry is a *genuine* feeling, but hitting doors or people is inappropriate.

Conflict resolution is therapeutic because the patient learns coping behavior and has a chance to be successful. Additionally, the patient can experience being treated with dignity and respect.

The need for conflict resolution is common in adolescent treatment programs. Discharge data summarized on a monthly basis by Dr. Dennis Hogenson indicates that an estimated 65 percent of young people who complete a treatment program require intervention from the program counselors, supervisors, or directors. Young people need this intervention because they come into treatment with so many unresolved and undiagnosed problems. The need for conflict resolution, however, may not lie with the patient but with an inappropriate treatment goal, inaccurate diagnosis, or unresolved family or emotional issues. In some cases, the same conflict resolution techniques need to be employed among staff members, either for inter-staff problems or unresolved staff-patient issues where an outside objective viewpoint is indicated. In any case, conflict resolution allows the staff to interact positively with the patient, offering suggestions, and seeking solutions, while allowing patients to take responsibility for their problems.

CHAPTER EIGHT

BASIC TREATMENT COMPONENTS

In this chapter, we will discuss the basic components of treatment including patient government, lectures, recreation, and volunteer involvement. We will look at how treatment teams work, and the qualifications counselors need. Then we'll focus on the types of treatment available, and how to set goals for individual treatment plans.

Counselors assume that patients can meet treatment expectations because patients are told repeatedly, "You are capable, and you can do it. We are putting the responsibility on you to follow through with the rules in a positive and appropriate way." At the heart of these statements lies the message that patients *can* complete what is expected of them because they have the ability and the tools to follow treatment guidelines. In this way, patients are treated with dignity and respect.

Conflict resolution comes into play when patients don't meet treatment expectations. For example, it is discovered in group that Lisa isn't working on her treatment assignments; instead she's involved in a backgammon tournament in the rec room night after night. The group confronts her and asks how she can take responsibility for catching up on her assignments. After admitting to herself that she knows she can't make progress if she doesn't do the assigned work, she decides it's more important to complete the overdue work than to continue in the tournament. This kind of conflict resolution provides patients with the opportunity to succeed at meeting treatment expectations. The following describes other ways of meeting treatment expectations.

Patient Government

Patient government groups, which can be established in each unit, serve several functions. They can promote responsibility and accountability by involving many of the patients in leadership and government positions. Group leaders take charge of the unit meetings and act as positive role models for other patients; unit secretaries record the minutes of meetings and post duties on the bulletin boards; other patients are elected to make coffee, clean lounges, and buy necessities for patients without shopping privileges.

Patient government groups also indirectly build self-esteem. Patients who provide leadership by acting as buddies to new patients on the unit, opening and closing meetings, and reading daily meditations, are modeling positive behavior. This helps them gain much-needed confidence and improves their self-esteem.

Patient-based Peer Pressure

This treatment component is developed in several ways. The patient government monitors patients by imposing penalties for breaking unit rules. If empty pop cans are left in a lounge, for example, patient leaders may stipulate that no pop be taken into the lounge for one day. Peer pressure is indirectly applied by "the buddy system" that exists between role models and new patients. Counselors encourage patient-based peer pressure by making statements such as, "You people work it out. You are capable, and we expect you to follow our rules." Directly or indirectly applied, peer pressure is critical in the operation of adolescent treatment centers for young people.

The Buddy System

An objective on an individualized treatment plan may state, "Be a buddy to two new peers to help you reach out to others." When buddies help others, they ultimately and indirectly help themselves.

Usually, before being a buddy, the patient must have had his or her First Step accepted by other patients on the unit, and this renews the patient's self-esteem. Thus, the buddy to a new patient can pass on a positive outlook about recovery. Buddies are screened before they're placed with new patients; they and the new patient usually have the same case manager. For easy coordination of activities and interaction, buddies participate in activities such as eating meals with new patients, familiarizing them with the treatment setting, and acquainting them with the A.A. program. Under the buddy system, the "older" patient has an opportunity to reach out, and the "newer" patient has the benefit of appropriate patient modeling. Both actions strengthen the use of peer pressure in the treatment setting.

Group Therapy

This component encourages patient discussion, sharing, and confrontation. Patients can discover who they are by listening to what others tell them about themselves. Patients' feelings, experiences, and behavior are reflected in the words of their peers helping them see themselves more accurately.

Group therapy also allows young people to share feelings they have often suppressed because of their drinking and other drug use. It helps patients see the defense mechanisms they use to hide their feelings. With the help of trained counselors and with honest input from peers, young people in treatment can begin to discover who they are by sharing and listening.

Confrontation

During confrontation, one person describes another's behavior but does not expect a particular outcome from the confrontation. When used correctly and appropriately, this communication process can bring about positive changes in attitudes and behavior. A staff member or a peer describes a patient's behavior by stating observable facts and follows by stating the feelings the behavior elicits. The confrontation should be made with care and concern, in a nonjudgmental and nonthreatening manner. A positive confrontation helps the patient see him- or herself more accurately. The following example of a confrontation could occur during a regular group session after the counselor asks the group if it is concerned with anything that occurred during the session.

Scott: I'm concerned about you, John, because I often see you by yourself.

John: (*A fairly new patient in the program.*) Oh, what do you know, anyway?

Scott: I just want you to know that I care. How about having a one-to-one with me after lunch today?

John: Oh, I suppose.

When confrontations can plant the seeds for change within patients by making them aware of how others see their behavior, they can be a positive element in adolescent and young adult treatment.

Daily Structure

The idea behind employing a strictly enforced daily structure during treatment is that chemically dependent people who are disciplined have less difficulty staying sober than undisciplined ones do. When adolescents and young adults use and abuse chemicals, they frequently lose routine in their lives. During treatment, structure, routine, and discipline help young people integrate structure into their lives.

The typical weekday in a young person's treatment program may begin with a 6:30 A.M. rising, followed by room and unit housekeeping tasks and breakfast. After breakfast, patients may attend a graduation ceremony, a lecture, and a group session, and then have lunch. Following lunch, time may be scheduled for school classes, a Big Book study group, a second group session, and free time. After dinner, a lecture, patient government meeting, and meditation time may be scheduled before bedtime. The structure is more leisurely on the weekend, and it changes to accommodate visits by doctors and psychologists, and testing sessions and conferences.

Some words of caution: although structure is extremely important for young people, it is possible to impose too much of it as well as too little. Successful treatment programs develop a schedule with a balance between structured activities and free time, realizing that such a balance allows patients to internalize what they've learned in treatment and helps them integrate it into their lives.

With structure comes compliance. Young people do not usually decide for themselves to enter treatment programs. They are most often placed there by concerned family or friends, and their first act of complying is staying in treatment. Peer pressure is applied to follow the rules and structure, thereby helping young patients meet treatment expectations. Some patients don't comply, and conflict resolutions and confrontations result. For the young person to be successful in treatment, complying turns into surrender.

Spirituality

Spirituality is an integral part of sobriety, healthy relationships, and credible treatment programs for young people. It is introduced to young patients as they study and practice the Second and Third Steps of A.A.'s Twelve Step program. Spirituality can be defined as "the quality of our relationship to whatever or whomever is most important in our life."[1] Some young people may initially believe spirituality has religious overtones. But when it is explained in the context of quality relationships and by the observation that "spirituality has to do with things which are the 'loves' of our life,"[2] young patients may understand that to incorporate spirituality into their lives is to enhance their growing sobriety. Many treatment programs for young people have resident chaplains to assist young people in defining concepts regarding spirituality and surrender and in creating their own understanding of their Higher Power. Chaplains also talk with patients about spirituality and its place in patients' lives.

Recreation

This component, absolutely essential in arresting chemical dependency in young people, should be integrated into the treatment plan. Young patients have high energy levels, and in recreation can begin to learn to have fun without using chemicals.

Young patients who have used chemicals over time have to be shown *how* to participate in recreational activities and *how* to have fun. Treatment staff can show patients how to have fun by participating in games and sports with patients and each other. Having fun together is a way the treatment team can model having fun for patients.

Different people like different activities. Some enjoy plays, art museums, or concerts. Others have fun playing softball or volleyball, or jogging or walking. What's important is that they are

- releasing their high energy levels, and
- experiencing changed behavior that enhances self-image and attitude.

Lectures

Young people learn in different settings and in different ways. Some learn more easily by reading, others by listening. Lectures, then, can be an integral part of learning. The goal of the lectures is to educate patients in a broad spectrum of chemical dependency issues. They may cover topics such as denial, reasons for failure, the disease concept of chemical dependency, and codependent relationships. In some programs, daily lectures are limited to one-half hour, the length of the average attention span of a young person in treatment.

Alcoholics Anonymous and Alumni Volunteer Visits

A.A. meetings are a regular part of many successful treatment programs. A.A. groups from nearby communities are generally available to come to treatment centers and conduct meetings. Often these meetings are young people's introduction to the Twelve Step program and an effective teaching vehicle for the Steps of A.A. Sometimes volunteers from community A.A. groups will take young patients to local A.A. meetings. The involvement of young patients with A.A. during treatment should continue after they leave the treatment facility and begin their aftercare plans.

Visits by program graduates are usually well received by young patients and meet a special need in treatment programs. Graduates may return to the facility on a regularly scheduled basis, perhaps once a month, and conduct A.A. meetings or informal discussions. They can speak with credibility to the patients about the kinds of issues they will face once they graduate and serve as living examples of successfully completed treatment.

Treatment Teams

Seventeen-year-old Mary has completed an assessment process. The diagnosis is chemical dependency; the recommendation, inpatient treatment. The entire staff–counselors, nurses, secretaries, and cooks–will influence Mary's treatment experience. Each person who interacts with Mary can help her behave constructively and adopt the positive attitudes necessary for her to begin recovery. Each encounter and conversation is of potential value in her continuing recovery after treatment.

It is important, therefore, that treatment team building include all personnel, from program directors, counselors, psychologists, and nurses to food service personnel and van drivers. The team concept suggests that each staff member is to be treated with the dignity and respect accorded the patients. While there are still disagreements among staff when the team approach is used, each person's opinion is valued and each person's contribution is recognized.

Most professionals in the treatment community agree that chemical dependency practitioners who work well with addicted adults will not necessarily have the skills to work effectively with young people, and should have specialized training. The State of Minnesota, as an example, requires thirty hours of specialized training in adolescent developmental tasks for chemical dependency counselors who work with young people.

Working with adolescents, especially in an inpatient setting, offers some of the greatest challenges in chemical dependency counseling. Given the unique developmental, family, and interpersonal issues that young people bring to treatment, daily personal interactions, combined with group therapy sessions, can be physically and emotionally draining for counselors. We will next examine the professional qualifications and personal qualities necessary for successful chemical dependency counseling in this challenging environment.

Counselor Qualifications

Program directors or the hiring team have a responsibility to evaluate the qualifications of prospective chemical dependency technicians and counselors. Technicians, who are counselor assistants, often work evening and weekend shifts in the treatment center. One of their important roles is to help patients develop goals. As much as counselors, they need to *like* working with young people and should feel comfortable talking with and listening to young people express their feelings and concerns. They need to enjoy interacting at the various emotional levels young people experience in treatment. Their ability to communicate empathetic and caring messages such as, "I understand your difficulty," "I can listen if you're ready to share," and "I'm available to help you" is important.

Counselors and support staff must believe that young people *can* be addicted to alcohol and other mood-altering drugs. Support staff should have basic knowledge of chemical dependency in young people and understand the dynamics of the illness. It is particularly important that counselors understand the signs, symptoms, and behavioral characteristics of chemical dependency in young people and recognize the issues that evolve from prolonged use and abuse. Treatment staff also need to understand the wide array of issues young people bring to treatment, and recognize how these issues become the major focus for treatment plan goals.

Those who work with young people also have to know their own personal boundaries. Young people in treatment are particularly vulnerable sexually; their words and actions often contain sexual innuendos. Counselors must have a strong standard of personal ethics and an understanding of themselves that will help them handle these situations. Young patients commonly form strong attachments to their counselors and even can become infatuated with them. What the young patients are really reacting to is the counselor's authority, caring, and empathy at a particularly vulnerable time when idolization is common. The astute counselor will recognize these feelings and be able to address the dilemma tactfully. The knowledgeable, caring counselor will not degrade the patient or take advantage of his or her vulnerability.

The educational qualifications for chemical dependency counselors vary from state to state: some states specifically require that the job candidate be a recovering person; others do not. The authors don't believe that one must be recovering to be effective. We do believe, however, that a job applicant who is recovering should have two or more years of sobriety before working as a counselor. Recovering people need to have resolved their own problems before addressing the problems of others. A counseling cliche holds that counselors can't take anyone beyond the point they themselves are at.

Usually the ability to work with chemically dependent people comes from a combination of education and experience. Whether the job candidate has a bachelor's degree in chemical dependency counseling or is a certified practitioner, the most important qualifications for the job are liking and understanding young people, knowing about chemical addiction, and understanding personal boundaries. These are critical to helping young people make positive lifestyle changes.

Interview Strategies

Interview questions are governed by state and federal nondiscriminatory hiring guidelines. Job candidates are not required to answer questions about age and race. Also inappropriate are questions that focus on whether the candidate is recovering or attends A.A. or N.A. The following questions are appropriate and useful to ask:

Question 1: I've read your job application with interest. Can you tell me something about yourself, your life, and your experiences in the past several years? [This kind of information helps the interviewer learn about the candidate's lifestyle and gives the candidate an opportunity to amplify information on the resume.]

Question 2: What is your definition of chemical dependency? [This question lets the candidate express personal and professional knowledge. The interviewer can contrast the candidate's philosophy with the treatment program's philosophy.]

Question 3: Do you believe that young people can be chemically dependent? [This question allows the interviewer to learn the candidate's philosophy regarding young people and addiction.]

Question 4: Do you understand what we do in this treatment program? [The candidate can share knowledge, and the interviewer can learn about the candidate's philosophy regarding young people and chemical dependency. The interviewer also can determine whether the candidate investigated the program's philosophies and goals.]

Each program director or hiring team has its own biases and list of personal characteristics that they value in counselors who work with young people. These may even include opinions about age-appropriate dress codes for employees, such as whether counselors need to dress conservatively or be allowed to follow adolescent fads and fashions. Assessments may also be made of the candidate's verbal and nonverbal (posture and handshake, for example) communication style. Treatment staff need to model the behavior, communication, and interaction skills they wish their patients to develop, and it is important to evaluate these qualities in a job candidate.

Types of Treatment

The purpose of treatment is to provide an approach or setting that will enable a young person to begin recovery from chemical dependency. After a team of evaluators has completed assessing a young person, they must carefully consider the type of treatment to recommend. Usually, the more pathological behavioral symptoms a young person has, the more structured the treatment setting should be. Regardless of all contributing factors, however, the team should consider other types of treatment before placing a young person in an inpatient facility. Treatment has evolved over the past several years to the point that many treatment options are available for young people.

Psychological and Pastoral Counseling

Treatment for some young patients involves attending weekly individual counseling sessions with a psychologist or a psychiatrist. Another treatment option is pastoral counseling – for both the individual and family. In either case, the counseling professional should know about chemical dependency and be able to recognize addictive behavior and symptoms. Young people are often sent to psychologists or psychiatrists for other problems only to have the primary condition diagnosed as chemical dependency.

Whether the setting is psychological intervention or pastoral counseling, the approach to take is to assess the young person's problems and needs and to prescribe a plan of action. The young person must agree with the plan and be held accountable to it. Referrals for further evaluation may be necessary if the young person doesn't appear to make progress in psychological or pastoral counseling.

School-Based Programs

Many high schools serve as referral and support sites. Trained chemical dependency specialists and counselors

86

intervene with students who come to school drunk, high on other drugs, or in possession of drugs and drug paraphernalia. Such students are often required to take drug education classes to learn about the causes and effects of using and abusing chemicals. Parents are encouraged to become involved when their child's drug problems are addressed. The chemical dependency specialist may require the student to sign a contract that commits the student to be drug-free and to participate in an abstinence program. If this is done, the student and the specialist should meet weekly to review contract terms. In many communities, groups such as A.A. and N.A. provide ongoing services and support to students who choose to remain chemically free. Students who do not respond to school-based intervention can be referred for off-site evaluation, and data collection can begin.

Outpatient Programs

Outpatient treatment, with evening and weekend lectures and group therapy sessions, is another type of intervention for chemically dependent young people. Outpatient treatment is less structured and less expensive than inpatient treatment. Patients do not live at the treatment center and are free to maintain their daily school or work schedule, or both. A typical outpatient schedule may require the young person to attend three evening sessions a week at a treatment center and two or three A.A. or N.A. meetings in the community. Twelve Step support groups are a vital component of the outpatient program; outpatient programs often require proof of attendance at support group meetings.

The young person must meet two criteria to respond successfully to treatment in an outpatient setting. First, the young person must come from a functionally healthy family. In outpatient treatment, family members become a part of the treatment plan. They provide support by interacting positively with the young person during selected therapy and group sessions and by helping the young person remain chemically free. Second, the young person usually must be in the early stages of the disease to benefit from outpatient treatment. During the early stages, the denial system is usually not as deeply ingrained. When it does become deeply ingrained, the young person finds it difficult to abstain from using chemicals, and this commitment to abstinence is essential in outpatient treatment.

The Treatment Plan's Goals

By conducting a comprehensive assessment, the treatment team can determine a young person's needs before the person begins long-term inpatient treatment. The team can distinguish among the young person's past needs, present problems, and post-discharge concerns. For example, unresolved grief is a past problem that may require psychotherapy. Denial of a problem with chemicals is a current issue that must be addressed in treatment. Renewing a relationship with a family member is a post-discharge concern. A primary function of the treatment team is to determine which issues will be addressed during treatment and which will be referred to other professionals.

The team and the young person should develop an individual treatment plan for each young person based on the critical needs the young person has that relate to chemical dependency. In addition, the plan should be designed to meet the patient's educational level and should also address the patient's level of denial. If a patient reads at the junior high school level, the team will need to write a plan that can be read and understood at that level. If a patient's denial prevents recognition of a problem with chemicals, a primary goal of the plan will be to help the patient recognize his or her chemical dependency. Basically, an individual treatment plan identifies a young person's critical problems, states goals that will solve the problems, and outlines objectives for achieving the goals.

Goals

Applying the principles of reality therapy, we have found it essential to require that patients define their own problems. Young people in treatment must acknowledge their responsibility as it relates to their placement in treatment, their chemical use, and their other current problems. They must also acknowledge how their problems have affected their lives. Taking responsibility for problems, then, is a prerequisite to making a commitment to developing goals for solving them. Taking this responsibility is the first step in a young person's recovery process.

After working with a counselor to identify problems that need to be addressed, the young person should be able to state his or her goals for improvement. Goals should be written in clear and direct language. Young people need not use psychological or treatment language. Negative statements should be rephrased into positive ones. The plan during treatment is to concentrate on short-term goals; long-term ones can be saved for the aftercare plan. The young person can focus on one or several goals, depending on the problem and on the person's cognitive level. It is most important, however, to keep the goals clear, understandable, simple, and attainable, and to set a deadline for achieving them.

The method for writing goals in treatment planning is to state the problem, the goal, and the objective. The objective, which is the method of putting the goal into action, must be developed by the young person. What follows are examples of problems, goals, and objectives often incorporated into treatment plans for young people. If this were an actual treatment plan, the patient's name would appear wherever the word *patient* occurs in the examples.

Problem: Low self-esteem resulting from feelings of guilt and shame.

Goal: Patient will begin to feel better about self by identifying existing positive qualities that will be useful for maintaining quality sobriety.

Objective: Patient will ask five peers to each state three positive things about the patient and share them in group; patient will keep a daily list of accomplishments and qualities that patient is proud of.

Problem: Patient's anger and defiance keep patient from accepting powerlessness, resulting in patient's relapse.

Goal: Patient will begin to identify how the need to control has resulted in relapse.

Objective: Patient will discuss issues of relapse in group; patient will listen to lecture on symptoms of relapse and discuss lecture notes with staff person.

Problem: Patient feels shame and embarrassment as a result of chemical use.

Goal: Patient will identify the existence of chemical dependency and recognize the belief and value conflicts that result from chemical dependency.

Objective: Patient will talk with three peers about experiences that resulted in shame that occurred while using chemicals; patient will share this new knowledge with counselor.

Problem: Patient feels pain and loss from growing up in a chemically dependent family.

Goal: Patient will identify three experiences of personal loss and will develop a plan to address the three experiences while in treatment and after discharge.

Objective: Patient will meet with a family counselor and relate family history to counselor; patient will write a story about the feelings experienced while talking with the counselor and share feelings in group.

One other step is required in the treatment plan process—commitment from the young person. This is obtained by establishing a deadline for meeting goals. Specific dates are essential. When the goal is attained, the counselor can divert the patient's energies to other problems that require redirection and change.

Working a Twelve Step Recovery Program

The treatment plan also must include a strategy for encouraging the young person to work a Twelve Step recovery program like A.A. Participation in an ongoing recovery program makes it possible for the young person to replace selfishness with humbleness. Consequently, Steps One through Five are incorporated into the individual treatment plan goals, and objectives are created to facilitate change.

- Step One discusses the importance of admitting powerlessness over alcohol and other drugs and helps the young person see how his or her life is out of control.
- Step Two focuses on developing spirituality that can lead to hope.
- Step Three requires a personal decision – to turn one's will over to the care of a Higher Power.
- Step Four requires the young person to take an inventory of his or her strengths and limitations.
- Step Five requires the young person to admit to a Higher Power and to another person how he or she has harmed oneself and others.

Young people who enter treatment are often irresponsible, isolated from family and friends, and completely engrossed in using and abusing alcohol or other drugs. They usually have stopped communicating with the people closest to them and lack self-confidence and self-esteem.

A positive treatment plan can motivate young people to return to the way they were before chemicals took charge of their lives if their turning to chemicals marked the arrest of a previously normal and positive development. After a successful treatment experience, young people can live a better life, one with enhanced self-awareness and increased maturity. Ideally, relationships with family and friends are restored; isolation diminishes; self-esteem is recaptured; and an improved lifestyle becomes a real possibility.

CHAPTER NINE

SEXUAL ISSUES IN
CHEMICAL DEPENDENCY

Women are currently abusing chemicals and becoming addicted at the same rate as men. What is not the same, however, is the rate at which they enter treatment. The ratio of men to women in treatment is four to one. This is true not only in adult treatment facilities but in treatment facilities for young people, which generally are equipped and staffed to serve young men.

Some treatment programs for young people serve both sexes, opting for either segregated or coeducational living arrangements. The heterosexual relationships that develop in such programs provide an opportunity for staff to examine sexual issues that may be significant in a young person's development and to the addiction itself. Often a pattern of harmful and at times abusive sexual behavior will be disclosed as a young person's history unfolds during treatment.

Treatment programs for young sexual abuse victims should create a nurturing framework of support that allows patients to build self-esteem and to share. In addition, such programs should endorse a philosophy of self-respect and promote staff modeling of positive behavior and attitudes.

Addressing Sexual Issues in the Treatment Plan

Treatment staff often employ special program activities to integrate young men and women in treatment. An ongoing concern when young men and women participate in treatment activities together is that they will become sexually active during the treatment stay. An important goal of treatment staff therefore is to promote companionship but discourage sexual relations. To this end, coeducational facilities can establish regulations that forbid sexual contact and specify immediate discharge for breaking these rules.

It is a challenge for staff to encourage interaction between young women and men while discouraging sexual intimacy; the line between the two is sometimes fine. Regardless, it is imperative to teach young people that relationships can be based on concern and caring, and that they can hug each other, and be otherwise physically affectionate, without having sex. The message that must come through is that young women and men can be friends and even love each other without engaging in sex.

A thorough patient assessment can alert the case manager to sexual issues that may arise during a young woman or man's stay in treatment. The treatment plan can then be written so that goals that address these issues are developed. In the healthy, affirming setting of a coeducational treatment unit, young men and women can be taught to have healthy relationships with each other as part of the treatment process. The treatment setting can serve as a testing ground where young people can practice appropriate interactions and communication skills.

Young people arrive at treatment programs with a variety of emotional problems. They often enter feeling ashamed, guilty, and emotionally dead. Many act tough, and some come with emotional scars that require years to heal. Others are so vulnerable that their emotions are nakedly exposed. Some exhibit forms of antisocial, defiant behavior. Regardless of the shape young people are in when they start treatment, the staff must approach them all with kindness.

During treatment, young people can learn about their soft side, gentle nature, and sensitivity. Through the staff's positive teaching and modeling, patients grow more comfortable with their gentler selves, and their physical appearances soften. They begin to develop a quality of self-pride observable by treatment staff and peers.

Male Sexuality

Treatment personnel are seeing an increase in the young men who report sexuality problems. Such problems range from dependency issues to sexual abuse in the family.

The big issue for many young men, however, is confusion about their gender role—what it means to be a man. Their confusion results from the conflict between what their family and society values as masculine behavior and their need for belonging and intimacy. Vulnerable to the message that being a man means being tough and macho, they may be violent with their male peers, girlfriends, or family members. One father, for example, told his son he wouldn't really be a man until he could beat up the father. Such attitudes and messages often reflect generations of physical abuse. In addition, these attitudes commonly produce a need in young men to dominate the young women with whom they attempt to have close relationships. In these instances, the need to dominate is a way for the young man to control his vulnerable feelings and to maintain a false sense of self-esteem.

Young men often bring much guilt and shame with them into treatment. Unresolved conflicts from the past, such as a girlfriend's abortion, the physical violation of others, childhood molestation, or homosexual acts exchanged for drugs, can produce a great deal of pain, which it is important for them to examine and begin to resolve.

Young men may especially question their sexuality with regard to homosexual behavior. Such behavior often puts them in conflict with their family's moral code and with religious teachings that label homosexuality a sin. Some young men believe that if they only had been taller, older, or stronger, if they were only more of a "man," these incidents wouldn't have happened. The stigma is sometimes overwhelming.

The Male Mystique

The feminist movement and sexual revolution of the 1960s and 1970s extended the range of acceptable behavior for women. Women can, for example, be more assertive than they formerly were and can pursue careers that were previously reserved for men. Men, unfortunately, have not made similar gains. Many young men see their behavior restricted to that of the tough, macho man so often portrayed in movies, television programs, and advertising. In these media presentations, the all-American man – handsome, tall, and muscular – is surrounded by beautiful women, or he is the center of popular male activities such as four-wheeling or football. He never feels fear, sadness, or isolation. As a result of these portrayals, young men continue to act out these roles. In treatment, however, some young men begin to discover the importance of addressing their sexual histories. They start sharing the pain related to chemical abuse and its effects on their sexuality.

Female Sexuality

Some contemporary women hold a traditional concept – that they are helpless without men. A society that promotes committed relationships and suggests that women need men to have their emotional needs satisfied teaches young women to be dependent on men. Society, through television programs and movies, shows young women that they should not seek

96

support from each other but from men. The concept of developing dependence on men filters down from the adult world and affects young girls who are exploring their sexuality. Young girls are taught how to tease and flirt to attract boys and men, and many spend a lot of time practicing this behavior. Moreover, it is not unusual for girls at an early age to develop jealousy and competitiveness over male attention. Young women in treatment get confused when they are confronted for flirting and competitiveness, behavior they were previously taught by peers and adults.

When alcohol and other drugs are combined with an adolescent's developing sexuality, the destructive behavior that results seems limitless. When drunk or high, for example, boys and girls easily become physically aggressive with each other. It is therefore common for girls as young as fifteen to be involved in physically abusive relationships as a result of chemical use and abuse. Sometimes a family's unhealthy behavior, the result of chemical use, is transmitted to its young members. When young people observe their parents or extended family members' aggressive, abusive behavior over time, it is only natural that they begin to act in destructive ways.

For young people as well as adults, excessive consumption of alcohol and other drugs often promotes sexual interaction. Young women who are drunk or high on drugs become more easily involved in inappropriate sexual behavior. Some exchange sex for alcohol and other drugs. This is not necessarily prostitution, but if it continues, prostitution can result. Some are raped. Others, as a result of getting drunk or high, cannot remember their sexual partners. When young women under the influence of chemicals have sex, it is usually unplanned. This often results in unplanned pregnancies, abortions, and prolonged feelings of guilt and shame.

Adolescents develop their value system at the same time they are engaged in sexual development and experimentation. When young people combine alcohol and other drugs with sexual behavior, their actions often conflict with their values. For example, a young girl may decide on the basis of her values that she is not going to have sex with her boyfriend because she wants him to respect her. If, as a result of intoxication, she has sex with him, she violates her value system. She may then decide that she isn't worthy of respect and continue the same inappropriate behavior. If this is the case, when young women arrive in treatment they may have had many sexual experiences and be faced with numerous issues regarding their sexuality.

Young Women's Support Groups

Although many questions about treating young women remain unanswered, it is clear that they are being successfully treated for chemical dependency in coeducational facilities across the country. This success notwithstanding, young women patients have special needs that require special treatment approaches. The women's support group is one such approach.

In many ways, without always making it obvious, young people confront issues about their sexuality and gender roles. In treatment, these issues can often be best addressed when young people interact in nonthreatening environments, such as women's and men's support groups. Here, young women and young men can share concerns about their sexuality and gender roles without distraction or embarrassment.

Because of the high ratio of boys to girls in treatment facilities for young people, it is important that treatment professionals take a protective stance toward young women. This may seem like a double standard, but many young women enter treatment physically battered and violated, making a protective attitude appropriate and providing a rationale for support groups. The groups give young girls the opportunity to take care of and assert themselves in treatment.

To best meet young women's needs, women's support groups are led by women counselors. To do this successfully, case managers and group facilitators must come to grips with their own competitiveness and sexuality before beginning to lead such groups. It is important for female staff to address these issues because they will be confronted by young women patients who don't know how to relate to female case managers except through competition. If the case manager allows competition to develop between her and a patient, potential for trust and acceptance is destroyed.

A truism among health care professionals is that it is impossible for health care providers to help patients through experiences that they themselves have not personally resolved. Therefore, health care providers in treatment settings need to address their own daily plans of recovery and self-discovery. This allows them to model appropriate attitudes and behavior for patients. It is impossible to overstate the importance of appropriate role modeling in treatment.

In the safe environment of a women's support group, young women can begin to identify and discuss their unresolved sexual issues. Likewise, young men in men's support groups are often more able to discuss their sexual concerns in the absence of women. In women's groups, young women are also free to identify and express feelings. They can learn and practice assertive communication skills and direct their attention to each other's immediate concerns. Also, the young women identify with each other. Feelings of aloneness and lack of trust are replaced by a sense of empathy and sharing.

Developing Positive Relationships

All too often young women in treatment did not have loyal and lasting relationships with other girls as they were growing up. The friendships they formed during their elementary and junior high school years may have dissolved once they began using drugs and drinking. Then, in the chemically dependent years, they often were jealous of and competitive with other girls, overtly seeking the attention of young men.

In a support group, young women begin to discover that competition and jealousy need not exist and that their needs can be met by other women, as they find that they can develop honest and trusting relationships with other patients in the group. As a consequence, they learn they do not have to seek male acceptance and nurturing to gain self-worth. When honest and accepting relationships develop among young women, they learn to trust each other and to accept others for who they are rather than for what they can do for them.

When young women start interacting in this way, they begin the long, slow process of developing self-confidence and self-esteem. They learn to work together, to teach and learn from each other, and to support each other. The passive victim disappears as does the flirtatious, competitive young tough. They discover that they have choices about how they act and who their friends are. They also learn that they can make positive, healthy decisions about using or not using chemicals.

The Chemically Dependent Young Woman: A Closer Look

Some young women in treatment will feel confused about unresolved sexuality issues. These are the young women who have experienced some form of sexual violation, physical violation, or both. This can have a bearing on their chemical dependency. The issues they confront include unplanned sex, rape accompanied by various levels of violence, unplanned pregnancies and abortions, and same-sex relationships. Young women may experience additional conflicts concerning their sexuality if they were raised in unhealthy families by chemically dependent parents. These young women frequently disclose sexual molestation, incest, physical abuse, and neglect.

The treatment setting is the first time that some young women have trusted anyone enough to reveal sexual issues and experiences. If they don't reveal these experiences, they may have difficulty beginning recovery or find it impossible to maintain sobriety. They may feel the need to drink or use other drugs to deal with their shame, physical and emotional violation, and feelings of abandonment. In fact, their chemical use may have masked these unresolved sexuality issues for a long time. The result is severely damaged self-esteem and continued use of drugs.

Very low self-esteem is almost always evident in young women who have experienced sexual or physical violations. Low self-esteem manifests itself in different ways. Victims of incest and child molestation suffer from feelings of shame and from a loss of power. These feelings cause self-hate and self-deprivation, and convince the young woman that she is intrinsically bad.

Young women experience loss of power as a direct result of sexual abuse. This doesn't necessarily result from the brutality of sexual assault, as is often depicted on television or in the movies. Nor does the loss of power necessarily result from the attacker's use of a weapon. Loss of power is the result of the invasion of the young woman's personal boundaries, which often begins when she is very young. It occurs when fathers, brothers, uncles, or neighbors misuse their power and sexually abuse or molest young girls.

The misuse of power is implicit in the attacker's verbal or nonverbal message to the girl: "You will consent because I am your parent. If you are a good girl, you will do what I tell you to do." The girl is caught in a bind: she cannot refuse because she has been taught to obey adults, but even as she submits she knows that consenting is wrong. Stuck in a situation where they have no choice, many young women become passive and can remain emotionally trapped within themselves for years. As a consequence of this loss of power, young women who have been sexually violated usually develop two defense mechanisms or coping skills to relieve their pain and help them deal with the world.

Complying and Submitting

Because their needs haven't been met by communicating their feelings and wishes, sexual abuse victims sometimes try to escape their pain by passively complying and submitting. They believe it is easier to remain quiet than to risk having their wishes ignored and rejected again. These young women are often nonassertive and lack decision-making skills. In addition, they are often people pleasers who avoid conflict and confrontation by readily agreeing with others on any subject. The only expressions they allow themselves are those that indicate that they think that everything – all events and other people – are wonderful. Their personalities are glass-like, brittle and fragile, mirroring the wishes of others, but capable of being scratched or shattered at the slightest conflict.

Anger

Anger is the contrasting defense mechanism or coping skill sexually violated young women employ. The anger lies near the surface of the young woman's subconscious and is indiscriminately directed at random events and people. This anger may lie dormant and unsuspected for weeks, months, or years, then suddenly flare up and unleash itself without good cause. If both anger and passive submission continue, they will mask the young woman's real condition by preventing her from recognizing her true feelings and dealing with the sexual abuse itself.

Young women eventually feel intense feelings of shame and guilt about inappropriate sexual encounters. Because the experiences have often been kept secret and unresolved for a long time, feelings of shame and guilt have grown until they permeate the young women's being. As a consequence, many young victims of sexual abuse develop self-destructive coping behaviors to help them deal with pain and shame. Some mutilate themselves, burning themselves with cigarettes, for example. Others attempt suicide. Still others develop unhealthy eating habits. Some may hide themselves behind excessive makeup or layers of clothing, or otherwise dress inappropriately. These destructive behaviors and defense mechanisms are often just an attempt to create a semblance of meaning or order in their lives.

Treatment Concerns

When young, chemically dependent women, who are victims of sexual abuse, enter treatment, first contact is usually with a female case manager. They typically respond to her in one of two ways: They may try to control the relationship by directing indiscriminate anger at the case worker. Or they may adopt a passive role, nonverbally indicating that they want their peers and the treatment staff to take care of them. Until the power issues are resolved, no trust can develop between patient and case manager. In addition, new patients, who do not understand the code of ethics and integrity of treatment personnel, may have difficulty believing they can trust the case manager. Moreover, boundary issues may surface whereby the case manager is seen initially as a threatening authority figure.

The primary task of treatment professionals is to arrest active chemical dependency and assist in the healing process by teaching a program of recovery. Young women in treatment need to be chemically free *before* their abuse issues can be addressed. Consequently, the treatment plan becomes the focus of recovery. Even if abuse issues are not directly addressed in treatment, staff members must observe certain guidelines when interacting with young female sexual abuse victims. These young women require the staff's respect for them as people, and its understanding of their feelings of shame, low self-esteem, and loss of power.

When to Make Referrals

Some patients' abuse issues are so complex that their needs cannot be met in a primary treatment setting. Others, however, can be treated. It is sometimes difficult to know why some respond well to treatment while others do not. Regardless, some young women may need to be referred to a hospital for intensive psychological care, while others can be referred for outpatient, community-based psychotherapy. Still others can be transferred to halfway houses to deal with issues related to sexual abuse.

Even when treatment is completed, because most of recovery takes place during aftercare, it is important that treatment centers encourage sexual abuse victims especially to attend A.A., N.A., and women's support groups after treatment. Attendance in these groups allows the healing process to continue after treatment is completed and keeps the sexual abuse victim who is recovering from chemical dependency in contact with other recovering people like herself.

When Treatment Doesn't Seem to Work

Each young women's treatment plan should contain short- and long-term goals that encourage the young women to develop healthy, normal interactions with young men and discourage overdependence. Some will continue to maintain this unhealthy overdependence and some even elect to leave treatment prematurely at the request of a man outside the treatment facility. Others choose to ignore treatment guidelines that prohibit contact between male and female patients. Still others spend too much time with one particular male patient and fail to complete their treatment goals. And some young women resume a potentially harmful relationship with a young man during aftercare rather than applying their energies to continued sobriety.

It is clearly not the treatment staff's job to overtly condemn a young woman's relationship with a man. The staff can, however, ask the patient in a nonconfrontational manner to evaluate both the positive and negative qualities of the relationship. There are many reasons the patient may resist this, but usually her resistance results from her low self-esteem. Society's messages about men and women, and the influences women's families have had, may keep young women from addressing their overdependence.

A young woman's overdependence on men can't be fully resolved in a chemical dependency treatment setting. It is also not the goal of chemical dependency treatment to convert all young women to a feminist viewpoint. The average thirty-day treatment stay cannot change living patterns developed over generations. Young women can best be served by being provided with a positive, helping, nonthreatening environment in which they can work on their abuse and other sexual issues.

CHAPTER TEN

WORKING WITH FAMILIES

When adolescents and young adults enter a treatment facility for diagnosis and evaluation, they bring with them their family's rituals, values, dynamics, and history. A patient's family provides important clues that will assist counselors in reaching appropriate decisions about young patients' diagnosis and treatment plan.

One would think that with close scrutiny, most families of chemically dependent young people would show many negative characteristics and destructive behavior patterns. It would seem likely that the interaction between mothers and fathers, brothers and sisters, and even uncles, aunts, and grandparents would reveal mostly conflict and be at least partially responsible for the addictive behavior. Such is not always the case.

Most families turn out to be basically healthy, and family members are usually happy, working, contributing members of society. A healthy family doesn't imply perfection, however; members of healthy families experience the illnesses, career crises, accidents, and losses that are part of living. It also can be expected that their lives will be disrupted and stressed as the children grow and move through the stages of adolescent development. But even as family dynamics and communication patterns change, these healthy families generally remain intact as they flex and adjust to these experiences.

Characteristics of a Healthy Family

Healthy families have diverse characteristics, and family therapists spend much time discussing the endless combinations of qualities that families exhibit. The research of family specialist and author Dolores Curran identifies fifteen traits of a healthy family.[1] In her research, Curran asked 551 respondents, all professionals who interact with families, to select and rank the fifteen traits they considered most indicative of a healthy family from a list of fifty-six suggested traits. The responses provide guidelines for self-evaluation and can help chemical dependency treatment centers and programs develop policies that encourage healthy family dynamics.

Trait One: The Healthy Family Communicates and Listens
Children in a healthy family are able to observe the open and honest communication between parents who share power and responsibilities. All members are encouraged to share feelings, to think independently, and to support each other. Members, because of their intricate relationships, recognize each other's nonverbal language and respond to each other's needs. Curran's research indicates that members of healthy families have the freedom to challenge each other in discussions because all members' opinions are valued. They are able to experience disagreements and know that they can reconcile.

Trait Two: Healthy Family Members Affirm and Support One Another
Each member is expected to support and affirm the other members. When mothers have careers outside the home, family members accept responsibilities at home to support her efforts. As sons and daughters become busy with jobs and

school, parents in turn support the children's efforts. Responsibilities change and adjustments are made when parents' jobs require travel outside the community. One member's goals and achievements are as important as any other's. But support for achievement doesn't turn into pressure to excell and perform. In addition, parents model self-esteem and set a positive mood within a healthy family.

Trait Three: The Healthy Family Teaches Respect for Others

Members of a healthy family respect each other's differences and decisions. Self-respect is taught and understood as real respect for oneself; each member is encouraged to develop strengths and talents. Parents in a healthy family create an environment in which respect for minority groups, other cultures, and neighbors and their property is encouraged through role modeling.

Trait Four: A Healthy Family Develops a Sense of Trust

This happens when husbands and wives role model trust toward each other and then provide opportunities for their children to earn trust. Allowing an eleven-year-old daughter to play with friends in an adjoining neighborhood is an example of providing an opportunity for a child to earn trust. Parents may write notes to their children explaining where they are when they leave the house unexpectedly to model dependability and thoughtfulness. Hence, the concept *trustworthy* becomes real through everyday interactions between parents and children. When a healthy family experiences broken trust among its members, the family can use the experience to teach that trust can be restored.

Trait Five: The Healthy Family Has a Sense of Play and Humor

When one young adult was asked to name her fondest childhood memories, she replied that some of the happiest times were family events at which her father and his two brothers were together. The three men shared laughter freely at family jokes and during family events and turned their laughter into loving family memories. Her choice of this out of all the possible events in her life, illustrates the importance of memory for the fun of it in family bonds.

Trait Six: A Healthy Family Shares Responsibility

In a healthy family, children learn that their responsible actions create self-esteem. All family members recognize that responsible behavior includes recognizing the other members' emotional needs. Moreover, parents understand their children's capabilities and set their expectations accordingly. Recognition is given for accomplishments; similarly, consequences are outlined for failure to act responsibly.

Trait Seven: A Healthy Family Teaches a Sense of Right and Wrong

Parents agree on important values, which they teach their children, setting clear, specific guidelines for enforcement. The parents help the children distinguish between appropriate and inappropriate behavior, and the children are expected to be responsible for their own moral behavior. The healthy family recognizes that not all people will agree with their morals; what is important is that the family has a strong moral base.

Trait Eight: Rituals and Traditions Abound in a Healthy Family

A healthy family treasures its stories and its members. The author of the book, *Roots*, Alex Haley reminds us that heritage is not just a roll call of our ancestors. He says, "Rather it is the *feeling* inbred in a family, what the forebears did, how they lived and coped, and what they left behind." The young woman who remembered laughter in family memories also was acknowledging her family's rituals and traditions.

110

Trait Nine: A Healthy Family Has a Balance of Interaction

Children readily observe that parents are equal partners in family relationships. Separate coalitions of family members are not condoned, and work and outside activities are not allowed to routinely infringe on family activities.

Trait Ten: A Healthy Family Has a Shared Religious Core

Integrating faith into daily family life and passing faith on to children in positive ways are two parts of the religious core. In addition, the religious core of a family nourishes and strengthens the family support system.

Trait Eleven: Members Respect Each Other's Privacy

This characteristic extends beyond respecting each other's choice of friends, time alone, and personal tastes. Privacy means that each family member is accepted and respected regardless of age, sex, talents, skills, or any other personal characteristic. The healthy family looks forward to the teen years of its children when rules can be negotiated rather than set by the parents. In addition, a healthy family lets go of the children, both physically and emotionally, as they leave home for education and careers.

Trait Twelve: A Healthy Family Values Service to Others

Members of a healthy family who value service to others demonstrate this by action rather than simply talking about it. Whether through car pooling, involvement in school functions or volunteer needs or service on community committees and task forces, family members are actively involved. But service outside the family requires a balance within the family. The family accepts a simpler lifestyle so time is created for service to others but at the same time, volunteerism is kept under control so that members have time for each other.

Trait Thirteen: Shared Meals and Conversation are Valued

This trait is related closely to Trait One, communicating and listening. Unfortunately, in today's world the time families spend together at mealtime is diminishing. Outside demands such as team practices and committee meetings, along with the ever-present television, are making unhealthy intrusions on family dinner table conversation. Mealtime is a time when family members can share achievements and frustrations, discuss their day, and teach values. Curran concludes that, "Families who do a good job of communicating make the dinner meal an important part of their day."

Trait Fourteen: The Healthy Family Shares Leisure Time

Balance is the key in sharing leisure time. Not all family members need nor want to be included in all family activities. To find balance, a healthy family prioritizes its activities, plans how it will use its time, and controls watching television. In addition, family members spend time with each other individually as well as within the family group.

Trait Fifteen: Admitting to and Seeking Help with Problems

Healthy families don't seek perfection—they admit their problems and get help. The healthy family realizes it's normal for families to have problems. In fact, some problems are anticipated. To help deal with normal kinds of concerns, the healthy family teaches its members coping skills and problem-solving strategies to use when appropriate. Sometimes the family seeks outside help from self-help groups like Al-Anon, Alcoholics Anonymous, Emotions Anonymous, parenting groups, and from counseling. Above all, the healthy family understands that having problems and solving them is a way the family can reaffirm itself and experience new growth and joy.

How Families Can Identify Chemical Abuse in Young People

With chemical dependency among adolescents and young adults one of the major problems confronting healthy families today, it's important that a family become informed about the effects of chemicals on young people. The seven signs and symptoms that follow can help families recognize behavior that may point to chemical use and abuse. Though these behavioral symptoms suggest possible chemical use, they are also indicative of other problems that a young person might be experiencing.

1. *Noticeable Change In School Performance.* The young person may demonstrate a lack of motivation by ignoring homework and skipping classes. Attendance may slip and tardiness become chronic. A sure sign is an unaccountable drop in the young person's grades.

2. *Sudden Change In Social Patterns.* For example, friendships dating as far back as elementary and junior high school may suddenly end as the young person begins hanging out with an unfamiliar crowd.

3. *Secretive Behavior about Friends and Activities.* Parents may not know their child's new friends because the young person is reluctant to introduce them or bring them home. The young person may lose interest in old, familiar activities, and may replace them with new, mysterious ones.

4. *Change In Family Relations.* The young person may begin to withdraw from family activities, fail to carry out family responsibilities, and stop communicating with some family members. Tension and conflict usually increase, and family fights about school, friends, and choice of lifestyle are frequent.

5. *Noticeable Change In Personality.* The young person vacillates between being quiet and being noisy and may

display several different moods within a short period. The young adult may also renounce goals, change interests, withdraw from responsibility, or show signs of depression including suicidal tendencies.

6. *Deterioration In Physical Appearance.* The young person's eating habits might change with sudden weight loss or gain. Clothes and grooming may change, either reflecting poorer hygeine or the current rebellious stance.

7. *Involvement In Legal Problems.* The young person may for the first time begin to incur traffic violations and be involved in vandalism, shoplifting, truancy, or running away from home.

Families Experience Grief and Stress

Families in which a young person is abusing chemicals may feel they have lost a son or daughter and often grieve the loss. Drinking and other drug use may have isolated the young person from family events, from open communication, and from day-to-day interactions with family members. Parents often report they have had little interaction with the young person for a number of months or even for a year or more. Kim, speaking in the book, *Young, Sober and Free,* says, "Alone I would sit in my candle-lit room, proceeding to stone my mind before going to bed and again before going to school. For a year I went on this way without much hassle. . . . I built brick walls, building them higher and higher . . . so as not to hear their [her family's] much too loud voices and over-dramatic lectures. Stone-faced, I hid behind those walls, denying and lying to their questions and accusations."[2]

Many families in which a young person is using and abusing chemicals experience the five stages of grief and loss described by Elisabeth Kubler-Ross that follow.[3] The stages outline the steps a grieving person experiences when someone close dies.

Denial

Families don't want to believe that a young family member is using alcohol or other drugs. After all, he is the star hockey player; she is the captain of the cheerleading squad. She is getting good grades in school and everyone likes her. How can this be true? The family ignores and disregards the evidence and denial becomes firmly entrenched.

Anger

Once they are confronted again and again with the evidence – the discarded drug paraphernalia, the everpresent Visine to clear red eyes, the mysterious capsules or powders incompletely concealed, and the telephone calls from unknown and uncommunicative "friends" – some parents conclude the adolescent *is*, in fact, using. Especially when the young person starts to come home at all hours of the night, often too drunk or stoned to remember his or her whereabouts or actions, the second stage of grief – rage and anger – sets in. Angry outbursts and arguing become the rule instead of the exception.

Bargaining

Parents begin bargaining with their child: "Please sit down and just talk with us. We'll try to understand. What can we do to help you?" "If you will stop using pot and stop hanging around with those friends, we will take a family vacation to Florida this year like we always dreamed of doing. Just come home when we ask, and let us know where you are going."

Depression

Bargains or not, drug-using friends are not discarded, the young person persists in the same destructive behavior, and isolation from family members continues. Family rules are broken and communication is nonexistent except for yelling and arguing. Parents may give up at this point. They become tired of *always* disagreeing with the young person. Fearful of what other family members will think about them and their children, and afraid to share their concerns with friends, pastors, or counselors, they become withdrawn. They begin focusing their attention on other events and projects if they have the energy, but often don't because stress has exhausted them. It is much easier for parents to withdraw than to continue arguing, fighting, pleading, or bargaining with the young person, much less do something meaningful for themselves.

Acceptance

Withdrawing eventually leads to acceptance, the final stage of grieving. The drug abusing young person is in control of family dynamics and interactions and levels guilt on other family members, who continue to withdraw. Some parents in this stage routinely complete their daily schedules, trying to ignore the young person's inappropriate behavior. Given the antisocial and isolating behavior that exists in families of chemically dependent young people, it is easy to understand how family members may feel grief, loss, and abnormal amounts of stress.

The family of a young person who has just begun treatment is usually under much stress. Family members have probably had to contend with a lot of inappropriate behavior related to chemical use, and may have had to deal with a young person's drug-related legal problems. There have more than likely been numerous family fights, arguments, and outbursts of uncontrolled anger and rebellion.

Even if the family has been passively enabling drug use by lying and covering up for a young person, its members are not free from stress. Many basically healthy families actually unintentionally enable the use of alcohol and other drugs because enabling often seems easier and less tiring than confrontation. After sleepless nights, family fights, and hours of pleading and bargaining with the young person, parents often find it less exhausting and less stressful to give in and give up. It is easier to say, "Johnny is absent because he doesn't feel good," than to say, "Johnny isn't in school today because he came home drunk at three A.M." A passive, submissive attitude toward chemical use and abuse is also less threatening to the family structure than the confrontive, assertive approach of intervention and possible treatment.

Families in Treatment

Addressing the needs of the families of young people in treatment has just begun. Much remains to be discovered and applied to family situations and interventions. What is known, though, is that just as each young person is unique, so each family is a unique unit. Patients and families change and grow at different rates. Given this, each family requires an individual response from the treatment community.

A common denominator among families, however, is the pain and distress that family members experience over the addictive behavior of their sons and daughters, brothers and sisters. Often the family has been in pain for a long time, so long that family members may not remember their happy experiences.

Just as young people are assessed for such things as chemical use, school achievements, and job history upon entering treatment, a thorough family assessment should also be a part of initial data collection. Treatment evaluators need to know if the family has a history of chemical abuse or if the young person is a first-generation addict or drug abuser. It's also important to know whether other family members previously have been assessed and diagnosed as chemically dependent or if their inappropriate chemical use is anecdotal and has not been professionally verified.

In addition to collecting information about the patient's and the family's chemical history, treatment personnel need to understand the family's values, rituals, and social backgrounds as they relate to alcohol and other mood-altering drugs. Some families do not serve or drink alcohol in their homes, while other families do so only on special occasions like Christmas and New Year's. Still other families believe it is permissible to con-

117

sume alcohol at any time and for any occasion. In some cases, all family members and friends are welcome to drink any kind of alcohol. Some families don't frown on drinking excessive amounts of any kind of alcohol but oppose use of other mood-altering drugs; for other families the opposite is true. Family rituals and mores can be as divergent as being expected to get drunk on your eighteenth birthday, to restricting alcohol use to religious observances such as a bar mitzvah celebration.

Families often bring unresolved issues into treatment; these issues may surface during a thorough family assessment. Family issues may include chemical use and abuse issues directly, but commonly cover a full range of concerns including conflicts between stepparents and stepchildren, jealousy between siblings, unresolved grief, conflict about living at home versus living independently, or emotional or physical abuse. These issues require varying levels of intervention and treatment.

Identification and Referral

The role of the chemical dependency counselor is not to become involved in intense family therapy. Chemical dependency counselors are not family therapists. Family counseling requires professionals specifically trained in family dynamics and interaction. This type of counseling takes time and only is effective after trust and rapport are established between the family members and the therapist. The role of chemical dependency counselors is one of identification and referral. Treatment counselors have the ability to help identify issues and pass on information to appropriate professionals.

Referrals depend on the needs of the family. Often they are made outside the treatment facility unless family counseling is available within. Another option is outpatient family counseling in the local community. Ideally, the professional the family is referred to will be educated not only in family counseling but also in chemical dependency and mental health counseling. Family counseling is a highly private and individual choice, and family's wishes should be respected.

Other kinds of family assistance include self-help groups such as Al-Anon, Alateen, and family therapy groups; educational lectures; financial counseling; and grief counseling. Treatment personnel may also recommend pertinent educational literature.

How Al-Anon Can Help

Al-Anon is one of the most effective programs in helping family members of chemically dependent people. Based on the Twelve Steps of Alcoholics Anonymous, Al-Anon teaches that family members need support in living and interacting with a chemically dependent person. Family members often suffer pain and become too involved in trying to help young people stop using alcohol or other drugs; parents especially want to fix their child's problems. In doing so, concerned people actually enable the young person's use of alcohol or other drugs to continue.

Through support groups and literature, Al-Anon teaches the principle of detachment. Its simple slogan is, When Things Go Wrong, Don't Go Wrong With Them. When young people are in pain, family members don't have to be in pain with them. When a family member abuses alcohol or other drugs and behaves inappropriately, others in the family do not need to take on the pain, blame, guilt, or distress. This principle teaches family members and concerned others how to help themselves, and in doing so, family members actually help the young person accept responsibility for his or her own life. This principle, however, can not be understood in one session. Detaching with love from the addicted person is a process that must be learned and practiced over an extended period. Changed attitudes and behavior can evolve with the help of a support group whose members share experiences and address the issues and needs of their children with dignity and respect.

Although a willingness to work on family issues in treatment is imperative for both the young person and the family, some family members choose not to become involved in treatment in

119

any way. Some do not want to change, while others deny the problem. Still others are threatened and are reluctant to discuss painful issues because they fear it will disrupt their lives. It can seem easier to maintain the existing condition than to deal with changed attitudes and behavior.

When treatment counselors work with resistant young people, they can often trace the patient's lack of growth to a resistant family member or to a family issue interfering with the young person's recovery. When a counselor discovers such an issue, it's important for the counselor to keep certain concepts in mind. Treatment personnel should avoid judging families or labeling them as lazy and lacking desire to work on issues. Families should not be addressed as chemically dependent or described as uncaring and unfeeling. Remember, families in treatment are under lots of stress and sometimes find it difficult to appropriately address current needs of their young people.

Some families whose young members are in treatment react out of strong feelings of fear, disbelief, and even embarrassment. Others are terribly concerned about the types and amounts of chemicals the young person has taken and about the drugs' effects. Some families have experienced loss and grief. Many still may be in shock or denial about their chemically dependent family member. Families experiencing these kinds of feelings should receive caring concern from treatment personnel; they need time to heal and grow. It is particularly helpful at this time for family members to become acquainted with the Al-Anon or Alateen programs. Moreover, when young people return to their families from treatment, they can especially benefit from the support of these groups. As families continue to seek help for themselves, they continue to help the chemically dependent young person.

Family Week

Many treatment facilities hold a Family Week for family member interaction. Families may be assigned a particular week during which all members come to the treatment facility for a variety of activities. Lectures, group sessions with treatment personnel, and group sessions with patients can help introduce family members to the process of recovery and educate them about the illness of chemical dependency.

As patients near treatment graduation, a family conference may be held with treatment staff, the patient, and family members. The purpose should not be to answer or even address all the questions and concerns family members have about the patient. The goal should be to educate them about the condition of the young patient and to make plans for aftercare involvement.

An excellent way to educate the family about the illness of their child or sibling is to begin with the patient sharing his or her drug history. In preparation for the conference, the treatment counselor can work with the patient, encouraging him or her to share as openly as possible. After the patient has shared drug history information, time is spent finding ways to help the patient continue recovery both during the remainder of the treatment stay and during aftercare. Aftercare planning plays an important part in the family conference; it is during aftercare planning that goals are established for quality sobriety.

The family conference may also be the first step in helping family members recognize that their personal problems affect the chemically dependent young person. It may become clear during the conference that other family members may need to deal with substance abuse or addiction issues themselves. For example, other siblings may also show behavioral symptoms of addiction, or a parent may demonstrate abusive behavior because of alcohol consumption. Because of this, some family members may perceive the conference as threatening and may resist being there.

It is critical, therefore, that the counselor take steps to create a positive, responsive setting and to establish clear guidelines and expectations. It is important that participants understand that each person has the right to his or her own opinion. Each member needs to respect the others, regardless of his or her feelings of anger or resentment. Family members should not be given permission to verbally attack each other; the family conference needs to be a safe place for family members to express real concerns and true feelings.

After establishing the initial guidelines, the counselor acts as a facilitator. The counselor now assists the discussion, encourages people to share, and moves conversation and sharing from one family member to another.

The counselor may restate ideas and request clarification. The counselor's primary goal is to assist family members in building positive interaction and communication in the family. In doing so, the counselor raises awareness of the issues and models useful communication skills. An inherent reward in working with chemically dependent young people and their families is seeing family members and young patients find answers to problems and begin to put order and happiness into their lives.

CHAPTER ELEVEN

POST-TREATMENT

A very small portion of the patients who graduate from treatment programs leave with the insight, determination, and courage needed for successful continuing recovery. Usually the past experiences and continuing needs of patients are so complex that well-developed aftercare programs are necessary.

Although effective treatment can arrest the illness of chemical dependency, it is usually a small part of any person's recovery. If percentages were assigned to treatment and aftercare, treatment would represent about 5 percent of recovery and aftercare about 95 percent.

Components of the Aftercare Plan

The difference between an afflicted life before treatment and a recovering life after treatment can lie in effective aftercare. The concerns in a young person's life that can be addressed in an aftercare program should be identified in treatment. These concerns include maintaining sobriety, usually with encouragement to become involved in a community support group, and find an A.A. sponsor. They can also include other issues such as educational priorities, vocational goals, and psychological counseling. These should be incorporated into the aftercare plan along with goals for just having fun while staying straight. Like the treatment plan, the aftercare plan should identify goals and methods for attaining them.

The No-Use Contract

Aftercare plans should include a no-use contract, an agreement the young person makes with the family. The no-use contract may state something like, "I will not use alcohol or other drugs; I will attend two A.A. meetings each week; I will become involved in an aftercare session; and if my way doesn't work, I will seek help." The no-use contract avoids the power struggle that can develop between the young person and the family regarding the continuation of treatment. It's also a way of helping young people get back into treatment if their methods don't work and they relapse.

Not all young people finish treatment; some leave prior to completing their goals. Aftercare plans are written for these young people also, and the no-use contract is incorporated into their plans. Obviously success is more likely to be achieved when young people complete their goals in treatment and finish their aftercare plans.

Outpatient Treatment

Several programs exist to help young people make the transition from the supportive but often confining setting of inpatient treatment to their relatively free but often troublesome home life. For some young people, outpatient treatment provides the structure necessary for making this transition positively. Outpatient activities may include attending group therapy sessions and family group meetings at the treatment center and A.A. meetings in the community. Consequently, outpatient programs can be considered one type of aftercare involvement.

124

When a treatment center is located in the community and young people have access to it, the aftercare program becomes an extension of the treatment program. Aftercare sessions are held at the treatment center, often one session each week for around twelve weeks. (Aftercare programs that are longer than twelve weeks may tie young people to the treatment center and prevent them from becoming involved in community-based programs.) During a twelve-week aftercare program, young people return to the treatment center and can begin the transition from the treatment setting to their homes and communities.

A.A. and Other Anonymous Programs

When treatment centers are located in rural or isolated areas or when clients travel to other states for treatment, it is often inconvenient or impossible for them to return to the facility for aftercare sessions. In this situation, aftercare goals and objectives should incorporate community-based resources into the plan.

Alcoholics Anonymous is still considered the best self-help group for arresting alcoholism. Founded in 1935 in Akron, Ohio, A.A. presently claims one and a half million members around the world. Successful A.A. members recommend attending weekly A.A. meetings on a permanent basis to remain chemically free. The principle of One Day at a Time along with attendance at meetings, reflection, and reading, provides the necessary support for millions of recovering people. Publications such as *Twenty Four Hours a Day*,[1] other daily meditation books, and pamphlets on many recovery topics are appropriate reading materials. The Alcoholics Anonymous Big Book, which relates the basic principles of the A.A. program and tells the stories of a variety of recovering people, has been the cornerstone of millions of people's recovery.

From its beginning, A.A. intended to help its members abstain from drinking alcohol. The Twelve Traditions and The Twelve Steps of A.A. provide the structure for the program and make it clear that A.A. is meant for alcoholics, although many people who attend the meetings have used other drugs as well. There are, however, A.A. groups throughout the country that do not allow people who are not primarily alcoholics into their meetings. Over time, people who used other drugs in addition to alcohol began entering A.A. programs, and the need for another organization became evident.

Narcotics Anonymous, founded in 1953, has incorporated A.A.'s Twelve Steps into its program, changing only a few words to make the Steps appropriate for N.A. membership. Every week at meetings throughout the United States, thousands of people report how living by the Twelve Steps has changed their lives. Consequently, Twelve Step programs like A.A. and N.A. remain the backbone of any effective aftercare plan.

Counseling

Some young people need more help in aftercare than A.A. or N.A. can provide. Their addiction is often related to underlying mental health conflicts such as unmanageable anxiety, character disorders, or irrational thinking. The aftercare plan, coordinated with mental health professionals in the patient's community, may include counseling by psychologists and psychiatrists, preferably those who have experience with chemically dependent young people. Chemical dependency counselors, social workers, and mental health workers can also help address specific problems such as eating disorders, family problems, and physical and sexual abuse. Many chemically dependent young people have these problems. They will do best when old conflicts at home, in school, on the job, or in the community have been resolved.

Halfway Houses

Halfway houses provide an interim living situation from the time a patient is discharged from a treatment facility to the time the patient returns home. They are an important part of recovery for some chemically dependent young people, and may make the difference for them between staying drug-free or not.

The primary purpose of halfway houses is to support the recovering young person's sobriety. Peer pressure, physical or sexual abuse in the family, or a young person's inability to resist chemicals are all reasons for placing a young person in a halfway house. Although some professionals who work with chemically dependent young people believe that placement in a halfway house should be required in aftercare plans, we believe a young person's specific needs should determine such placement. Some young people have a lot of difficulty refusing chemicals and adjusting to their former environment. If peer pressure to use drugs or drink is strong, a young person who has difficulty with peer pressure will benefit from placement in a halfway house.

The average stay in a halfway house is three to six months. During this time residents attend school, work in the community, or do both. Halfway houses are usually staffed by house managers and chemical dependency counselors, who provide ongoing supervision and structured programs in counseling, recreation, nutrition, and spiritual development.

Like most treatment programs, halfway houses are licensed facilities whose services may be covered by medical insurance plans. They need to meet state guidelines and to maintain accurate records. Although many people accept halfway houses in their neighborhoods, some don't want them. They may petition to keep them out because they are fearful about neighborhood safety. The truth is that most halfway houses have structured rules that make the environment safe for the people in the halfway house and for people in the community.

Having Fun without Chemicals

Young people spend a lot of their leisure time in social activities. One part of aftercare for chemically free young people is figuring how to have fun without using chemicals. Although there is usually time for social interaction at A.A. and N.A. meetings, it doesn't begin to amount to the time young people previously spent using chemicals. Even young people who realize that chemicals created serious problems for them in the past, and that the consequences of drinking and using drugs were not fun, need to be taught that there are ways to have fun besides getting high. To do this, most inpatient treatment programs offer activities that help integrate recreation into free time. It's important that this concept be carried into aftercare.

Drug-Free Nightclubs

Drug-free nightclubs are meeting places that support recovering people by serving only nonalcoholic beverages. The most important thing they offer is companionship. In addition, many of them have bands or some type of music, pinball machines, video games, and food. Their success in helping young people remain chemically free varies. Some people who are new to recovery find that the clubs remind them of bars, making it easy for them to slip back into drinking and using other drugs.

Support Groups in Schools

Support groups are necessary for young people when they leave treatment and return to school and their friends. Like the halfway house, the school support group may make the difference in some young people's ability to stay drug-free. Groups do this by providing support in school, where peer pressure to use chemicals is frequently very strong. Support groups are usually led by teachers or counselors who understand chemical dependency or want to learn about the recovery process. Group facilitators must be knowledgeable about recovering young people's needs and be able to demonstrate group process skills. Group members exchange phone numbers, confide in each other, and give and receive positive feedback. Confidentiality is essential in any support group, especially those held in high schools and junior highs. Too often these groups become ineffective because members break shared confidences.

School administrators have developed various policies concerning support groups. Some schools give academic credit to encourage recovering people to attend; others let students leave class to attend meetings; some let groups use the school before or after school hours. Support groups should not be repositories for students being punished for drinking or using other drugs on school grounds. Recovering young people use groups to get support from their recovering peers; they shouldn't be in groups with students who are being punished and don't have a desire to stop using or drinking.

Continuing Spiritual Growth

Halfway houses, A.A., N.A., professional counseling, and recreation without chemicals—all play an important part in a young person's aftercare plans. We believe there is an additional component to successful aftercare—continuing spiritual growth and development. In our experience, patients need to develop a daily awareness of their Higher Power. Those who do best when they leave treatment develop a growing sense of the connection between the quality of their personal spiritual lives and the quality of their lives at home, at work, and in their community. Living well requires more than the satisfaction of material and physical needs. Therefore, we encourage all patients to look to their Higher Power for guidance in living their lives One Day at a Time.

ENDNOTES

Foreword

1. "Next Steps in the Evolution of Chemical Dependency Care in Minnesota," *Citizen's League Report* (Approved by the Citizen's League Board of Directors 13 June 1980), 22.

Chapter One

1. Letter to Dr. Jung, quoted in *Pass It On – The Story of Bill Wilson and How the A.A. Message Reached the World* (New York: Alcoholics Anonymous World Services, Inc., 1984), 381–86.
2. *Alcoholics Anonymous* (The Big Book), Third Edition (New York: Alcoholics Anonymous World Services, Inc., 1976), 315.

Chapter Two

1. Tom Bouchart and Matt McGue, "Adjustment of Twin Data for the Affects of Age and Sex," *Behavior Genetics*, 14, No. 4 (January 1984), 325.
   Tom Bouchart, "Do Environmental Similarities Explain the Similarities in Intelligence of Identical Twins Reared Apart," *Intelligence*, 7, No. 2 (April-June, 1983), 175.

Chapter Three

1. William Glasser, Dennis Hogenson's interview with, training session in reality therapy, Santa Monica, Calif., 12 June 1977.

Chapter Four

1. Daniel J. Levinson, *Seasons of a Man's Life* (New York, Ballantine Books, Inc.,1978), 61.
2. Barbara M. and Philip R. Newman, *Development Through Life: A Psychosocial Approach* (Homewood, Ill.: The Dorsey Press, 1979).
3. Mollie S. Smart and Russell C. Smart, *Adolescents Development and Relationships* (New York: The Macmillan Publishing Co., Inc.,1973), 70.
4. Ibid., 187.

Chapter Five

1. Richard O. Heilman, *Early Recognition of Alcoholism* (Center City, Minn.: Hazelden Educational Materials, 1973), 9–11.
2. Ibid., 7–8
3. Ibid., 7.
4. Ibid., 8.
5. G. A. Henly and K. C. Winters, *Personal Experience Inventory* (Unpublished manuscript).
6. Ibid.
7. Taken from questions prepared by Dr. Robert B. Seliger for use at Johns Hopkins University Hospital, Baltimore.
8. J. George Strachan, *Alcoholism: A Treatable Illness. An Update for the 80's* (Center City, Minn.: Hazelden Educational Materials, 1982), 136A.

9. *Alcoholics Anonymous* (The Big Book), Third Edition (New York: Alcoholics Anonymous World Services, Inc., 1976), 30.

Chapter Eight

1. Paul E. Bjorklund, *What Is Spirituality?* (Center City, Minn.: Hazelden Educational Materials, 1983), 3.
2. Ibid., 6.

Chapter Ten

1. Dolores Curran, *Traits of a Healthy Family* (Minneapolis: Winston Press, 1983). Reprinted with permission of Dolores Curran.
2. Shelly Marshall, *Young, Sober and Free* (Center City, Minn.: Hazelden Educational Materials, 1983), 49.
3. Elisabeth Kubler-Ross, *Death, The Final State of Growth* (Englewood Cliffs, N.J., Prentice Hall, 1975), 10.

Chapter Eleven

1. *Twenty Four Hours a Day* (Center City, Minn.: Hazelden Educational Materials, 1975).

GLOSSARY OF TERMS

To help our readers better understand the context in which certain terms and phrases are used by us, we offer the following glossary of terms:

ACTING OUT. This term is used usually with specific reference to adolescent and young adult behavior characterized by impulsiveness, rebelliousness, and opposition to adult control and authority. Some acting out in adolescence is normal. We are, however, referring to abusive, self-defeating, and injuriously excessive acting out that often includes chemical abuse and dependency.

ACUTE BEHAVIOR. This term involves a degree of human behavior that has become excessive. A crisis situation is implied. Behavior of this type will be recognized by most observers as presenting a danger to the person(s) involved.

AFTERCARE. This term means a planned program of recovery experiences intended to strengthen the treatment program. Aftercare planning might include regular A.A. attendance, halfway house placement, counseling, or psychotherapy. In all cases the planned experiences happen after the treatment program has been completed.

BIPOLAR DEPRESSION. This term describes a pattern of psychological distress in which depression cycles between two extremes of expression. The patient might show symptoms of depression including a lack of energy, diminished hope and pessimism about the future, problems with sleep or appetite, et cetera. Conversely, the patient might also have periods of excessive energy, impulsiveness, delusional thinking, impulsive and imprudent financial dealings, and hyper-verbal or hypermotor responses more typically thought of as manic or hypomanic behavior.

CARE PROVIDERS. This term is used by us to refer to all of the people in the treatment program, or elsewhere in the patient's life, who act directly to provide for the patient the necessary elements in the patient's physical, academic, spiritual, and social development. Care providers can be parents, teachers, employers, friends, and others, in addition to the patient's counselors working within the treatment program itself.

CARE SPECIALISTS. This term describes people within the treatment program who function in very well-defined and specialized categories. It is the nature of the duties performed that designates specific care specialists. Examples include intake specialist, aftercare planner, nurse, physician, recreational specialist, psychologist, et cetera.

CHEMICAL DEPENDENCY. The use of mood-altering chemicals characterized by repeated, unsuccessful efforts to control use and continued use in spite of the evidence of related harmful consequences. *Nondependent chemical abuse or misuse* is characterized by repeated use manifesting problematic consequences with no apparent significant loss of control.

DELUSIONAL. We use this term to mean behavior that does not seem to be fully grounded in reality or in common human perception. Delusional refers to an element of mistaken belief or observation, sometimes required by the patient to maintain self-defeating or injurious activities such as chemical dependency, negative relationships, or neurotic activities.

DETERMINANTS. This is a very general term used by us in attempting to assign meaning to separated segments of behavior. Determinants highlight specific elements of behavior. As an example, determinants in defining an addictive condition might include compulsion, abuse, and negative consequences of use.

ENDOGENOUS. This is a term used most frequently by psychologists, psychiatrists, and physicians to refer to elements in behavior or psychopathology that exist within the physical functioning of the patient. An example would be depression related to a genetic predisposition by the patient. Other examples could include biochemical and hormonal changes that result in the appearance of depression or similar pathological conditions.

MINNESOTA MULTI-PHASIC PERSONALITY INVENTORY (MMPI). The MMPI is the most widely used personality test in the Western world. This is a specific paper and pencil personality testing instrument developed at the University of Minnesota by Hathaway and McKinley and first copyrighted in 1943. The test is currently published by the University of Minnesota Press and distributed by National Computer Systems Inc. The test contains 566 short statements which a person is asked to answer true or false. The results of the test show four validity scales, ten traditional clinical scales, and numerous new and experimental scales. The four validity scales measure the number of questions actually responded to, the degree of objectivity and truthfulness of the respondent, the responsibility and consistency of the respondent as a testing subject, and the extent to which the subject was able to objectively identify with his or her behavior. The ten clinical scales provide a profile of personality pathology utilizing diagnostic categories (for example, depression, hysteria, psychopathic deviation, masculinity-femininity, paranoia, and so on.) One of the experimental scales is the MacAndrew's scale which appears to measure addictive tendencies within the personality.

PROJECTION. This is an unconscious tendency to assign to others some of our own negative thoughts, feelings, or behavior (for example, anger, aggressiveness, lust).

PSYCHOLOGICAL DEFENSE SYSTEM. This term refers to common behaviors of people including chemical dependency patients intended to defend the ego or sense of self from stress and painful insights. Defense mechanisms are largely unconscious in the sense that the person using them is typically not aware of his or her behavior. Examples include denial, rationalization, projection, reaction formation, and sublimation.

PSYCHOTROPIC. This term is used by us to refer to a group of prescribed medicines that act to change or modify human behavior. Examples of psychotropic medications include antidepressants, antianxiety medications, and antipsychotic medications.

REACTION FORMATION. This is a psychological process wherein the person overresponds to an unconscious need or drive by behaving the opposite way. Typically the person is not aware that he or she is doing this. As an example, an unconscious compulsion for alcohol abuse could be expressed in actively lobbying for stricter drunk driving laws.

RORSCHACH TEST. This is one of many personality tests included in the category called *projectives*. The test includes ten paperboard cards approximately 6 x 10 inches in size. One-half of the cards are in black and white. The other half combine black ink with lightly colored pastels. All of the cards contain abstract design content of varying degrees of complexity. An elaborate scoring system for a patient's responses is used by the psychologist to create a personality profile for the patient.

BIBLIOGRAPHY

Alcoholics Anonymous (The Big Book), Third Edition. New York: Alcoholics Anonymous World Services, Inc., 1976.

Anderson, Daniel J. "A.A.'s 12 Steps Will Work for Problems with Food, Drugs." *Minneapolis Tribune*, 1987.

The Association of Junior Leagues, Inc. "Woman to Woman." New York.

Beattie, Melody. *Codependent No More*. Center City, Minn.: Hazelden Educational Materials, 1987.

Bjorklund, Paul E. *What Is Spirituality?* Center City, Minn.: Hazelden Educational Materials, 1983.

Bouchart, Tom and Mat McGue. "Adjustment of Twin Data for the Affects of Age and Sex." *Behavior Genetics*, vol. 14, no. 4 (January 1984): 325–43.

Bouchart, Tom. "Do Environmental Similarities Explain the Similarities in Intelligence of Identical Twins Reared Apart?" *Intelligence* vol. 7, no. 2 (April-June 1983): 175–84.

Curran, Dolores. *Traits of a Healthy Family*. Minneapolis: Winston Press, 1983.

Dollard, J. and N. Miller. *Frustration and Aggression*. New Haven, Conn.: Yale University Press, 1939.

Glasser, William. *Reality Therapy: A New Approach to Psychiatry*. New York: Harper & Row, 1975.

Hazelden Quality Assurance. Center City, Minn.: Hazelden Educational Materials, October-December 1987.

Kubler-Ross, Elisabeth. *Death: The Final Stage of Growth*. Englewood Cliffs, N.J.: Prentice Hall, 1975.

Levinson, Daniel J. *Seasons of a Man's Life.* New York, Ballantine Books, Inc., 1979.

Marshall, Shelly. *Young, Sober and Free.* Center City, Minn.: Hazelden Educational Materials, 1983.

Narcotics Anonymous. Van Nuys, Calif.: World Services Office, Inc., 1982.

Newman, Barbara M. and Philip R. *Development Through Life: A Psychosocial Approach.* Homewood, Ill.: The Dorsey Press, 1979.

Perkins, William Mack and Nancy McMurtrie-Perkins. *Raising Drug-Free Kids In a Drug-Filled World.* Center City, Minn.: Hazelden Educational Materials, 1986.

Porterfield, Kay Marie. *Familiar Strangers.* Center City, Minn.: Hazelden Educational Materials, 1984.

Smart, Mollie S. and Russell C. Smart. *Development and Relationships,* 2d ed., vol. 3. New York: Macmillan Publishing Co., Inc.,1978.

Strachan, J. George. *Alcoholism: Treatable Illness. An Update for the 80's.* Center City, Minn.: Hazelden Foundation, 1982.

U.S. Surgeon General's Report. "Smoking and Health – A Comparison Bibliography." Biomedical Information Guide Services, vol. 3.

Winters, K. C., and G. A. Henly. *Personal Experience Inventory.* Los Angeles: Western Psychological Services, 1988.

INDEX